We recently lost our beloved pet "Bear," who was not only our best and dearest friend but also the "Vice President of Sunshine" here at Atlantic Publishing. He did not receive a salary but worked tirelessly 24 hours a day to please his parents. Bear was a rescue dog that turned around and showered myself, my wife, Sherri, his grandparents

Jean, Bob, and Nancy, and every person and animal he met (maybe not rabbits) with friendship and love. He made a lot of people smile every day.

We wanted you to know that a portion of the profits of this book will be donated to The Humane Society of the United States. —*Douglas & Sherri Brown*

The human-animal bond is as old as human history. We cherish our animal companions for their unconditional affection and acceptance. We feel a thrill when we glimpse wild creatures in their natural habitat or in our own backyard.

Unfortunately, the human-animal bond has at times been weakened. Humans have exploited some animal species to the point of extinction.

The Humane Society of the United States makes a difference in the lives of animals here at home and worldwide. The HSUS is dedicated to creating a world where our relationship with animals is guided by compassion. We seek a truly humane society in which animals are respected for their intrinsic value, and where the human-animal bond is strong.

Want to help animals? We have plenty of suggestions. Adopt a pet from a local shelter, join The Humane Society and be a part of our work to help companion animals and wildlife. You will be funding our educational, legislative, investigative and outreach projects in the U.S. and across the globe.

Or perhaps you'd like to make a memorial donation in honor of a pet, friend or relative? You can through our Kindred Spirits program. And if you'd like to contribute in a more structured way, our Planned Giving Office has suggestions about estate planning, annuities, and even gifts of stock that avoid capital gains taxes.

Maybe you have land that you would like to preserve as a lasting habitat for wildlife. Our Wildlife Land Trust can help you. Perhaps the land you want to share is a backyard— that's enough. Our Urban Wildlife Sanctuary Program will show you how to create a habitat for your wild neighbors.

So you see, it's easy to help animals. And The HSUS is here to help.

THE HUMANE SOCIETY OF THE UNITED STATES.

2100 L Street NW • Washington, DC 20037 • 202-452-1100
www.hsus.org

The Complete Guide to

Beekeeping

for Fun & Profit:

Everything You Need to Know Explained Simply

With Cindy Belknap

THE COMPLETE GUIDE TO BEEKEEPING FOR FUN & PROFIT:
EVERYTHING YOU NEED TO KNOW EXPLAINED SIMPLY

Copyright © 2010 Atlantic Publishing Group, Inc.
1405 SW 6th Avenue • Ocala, Florida 34471 • Phone 800-814-1132 • Fax 352-622-1875
Web site: www.atlantic-pub.com • E-mail: sales@atlantic-pub.com
SAN Number: 268-1250

Library of Congress Cataloging-in-Publication Data

Belknap, Cindy, 1952-
  The complete guide to beekeeping for fun & profit : everything you need to know explained simply / Cindy Belknap.
      p. cm.
  Includes bibliographical references and index.
  ISBN-13: 978-1-60138-362-4 (alk. paper)
  ISBN-10: 1-60138-362-2 (alk. paper)
  1. Bee culture. 2. Bees. I. Title.
  SF523.B394 2010
  638'.1--dc22
                          2009053851

Printed in the United States

PROJECT MANAGER: Nicole Orr • norr@atlantic-pub.com
PEER REVIEWER: Marilee Griffin • mgriffin@atlantic-pub.com
FINAL EDITOR: Sheila Reed
ASSISTANT EDITOR: Angela Pham • apham@atlantic-pub.com
INTERIOR DESIGN: Samantha Martin • smartin@atlantic-pub.com
FRONT COVER DESIGN: Meg Buchner • meg@megbuchner.com
BACK COVER DESIGN: Jackie Miller • millerjackiej@gmail.com

Printed on Recycled Paper

Dedication

To all beekeepers, young and old. If you are planning your first hive, you are embarking on a miraculous journey that will provide a lifetime of enjoyment. If you cannot even remember how many hives you have had over the years, you know what I mean.

— Cindy Belknap

Table of Contents

Chapter 2: What You Need to Know About Beekeeping   61

Chapter 3: Working the Hive   93

Chapter 8: Cooking With Honey   199

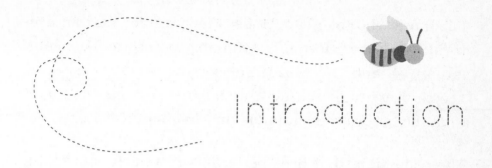

Introduction

Beekeeping: Where else can you find thousands of sisters working together in perfect harmony under one roof?

Bee enthusiasts become beekeepers for a variety of reasons, but most admit their unadulterated fascination comes from what bees are capable of doing. New beekeepers also mention the unique aspects of the hobby, its educational assets, and the chance to get back to nature as to reasons they enjoy the hobby. And then there are those who extol the financial virtues of beekeeping. One beehive will usually bring in more honey than one person could possibly use, and it is not hard to imagine all the ways to sell your gorgeous crop of honey. Homegrown, organic honey is a sought-after commodity, but becoming an apiarist, which is the formal name for a beekeeper, is so much more than bee stings, wax, and honey.

For those who take care of bees for pure joy and amusement, you are performing a valuable service to your community — and the world. The simple act of beekeeping keeps diversity in the flora and fauna, insects, soil, and even the herbivorous animals that frequent the area.

The pollination that bees perform is extremely important. Without their hard work, the world would be without many species of plants, fruits, and flowers. Honey bees provide the pollination for more than 80 percent of the fruit, vegetable, and flowering plants in existence. They pollinate crops used to feed cattle and other meat and dairy animals. Honey bees also contribute at least $150 million in honey annually, plus the estimated $50 million in beeswax used in cosmetics, candles, and other products. A Cornell University study estimated that honey bees pollinate more than $14 billion worth of seeds and crops in the United States each year. Some crops are almost singularly dependent on the honey bee for pollination.

Beekeeping is not for everyone; it requires hard work. There are bee boxes (supers) to put together, pests to be monitored and treated, and bees to be fed and managed. Beekeeping is a hot, sweaty, and thoroughly enjoyable hobby, even with the occasional sting or two.

This is a hobby with living creatures — creatures that perform a very important job for our society. Always treat bees with the respect they deserve.

Beekeeping is more than gathering honey. Here you will learn not only what is needed to take care of a colony of productive bees, but also the troublesome areas that all beekeepers face. Disease and infection affect all living creatures, and bees are no exception. The diseases that affect bees are especially troublesome because they impact honey, wax, and all other elements of beekeeping. Disease can wipe out an entire colony and destroy hope for profit. Knowing the prospective diseases is an important part of beekeeping.

Hive life is not without its dramas. Bees have been known to pick up and fly away from their hive. If the colony stays, the queen might disappear, or perhaps another colony might decide they want your honey and may begin robbing it.

There is also a business aspect to beekeeping. Pollination and honey are not the only way bees contribute to human society. Their propolis, wax, larvae, and venom are all important commodities. Each one has its own distinctive characteristic when it comes to marketing and distribution.

So, prepare for an adventure of a lifetime, because beekeeping is life-altering. You will become infatuated with your bees and develop a relationship with them and with nature. It is a learning adventure with an environment like no other.

Chapter 1
Beekeeping Basics

All About Bees

Honey bees belong to the largest order of insects known as Hymenoptera, which translates to "membranous wings," and includes sawflies, wasps, bees, and ants. The scientific name for a honey bee is *Apis mellifera*. They are able to provide a social service with their pollination, honey production, and propolis, which is a mixture that bees collect from tree buds to fill in open gaps in their hives. Although the number of new beekeepers is on the rise, the number of honey bee colonies is on the decline. In 2006, there were 6 million registered colonies, but by 2009 the population dropped to 2.4 million. This phenomenon, called colony collapse disorder (CCD), was first reported in 2006, although recent studies suggest it may have begun as early as 2004. The main characteristic of CCD is a sudden loss of a colony's adult bee population, with no dead bees found inside or near the hive. Although extensive research has been conducted on this plight, no singular reason has been discovered as the cause. Scientists have narrowed down the possibilities to include pesticides in our environment, diseases, and poor honey bee management, to name a few. However, the treatment for this serious disorder has not been discovered. But although it might not seem like a good time to start this new venture, in reality, it is the best time. Honey bee researchers are encouraging people to take up beekeeping to help reverse this decline in population — properly managed hives have a much better chance of survival than hives in the wild.

The Latest Buzz on a Vanishing Species

By Nedda Pourahmady

Bees, a vital part of the insect population, are dying out at rapid rates. In the beginning of 2007, news reports surfaced when alarmed beekeepers discovered that half of their bees had disappeared. The queen bee and a few newborns were the only existing bees found in the hives.

Provided by FDACS-DPI (University of Florida)

Because honey bees are essential to the pollination of food crops, their decline has a widespread impact. Honey bees contribute to $15 billion worth of agricultural products. Every year in February, beekeepers traveling to California bring more than 1 million hives containing approximately 40 billion honey bees. In a matter of weeks, the bees work hard to pollinate 80 percent of the world's almond crop, which amounts to about $1 billion in exports.

As a result of colony collapse disorder (CCD), food and honey production have been disrupted significantly. The primary victims of the disorder are domestic, commercial honey bees. Bees transferred around for crop pollination also seem to be affected.

However, this does not mark the beginning of vanishing bees. In 1915, beekeepers in several states experienced significant reductions in bee counts. The direct cause for CCD is unknown, but there are some theories attempting to explain the phenomenon.

Many bees encounter stress from extended periods of pollination. These overworked insects may develop a weak immune system, making them more vulnerable to external pathogens and deterring their ability to navigate. Furthermore, varroa and tracheal mites may introduce an unknown virus to bees.

Fortunately, the U.S. Department of Agriculture has implemented a plan to fight against CCD. In 2007, the CCD Steering Committee was formed. The group, comprising representatives from other government agencies, academia, beekeepers, and professional organizations, developed the Colony Collapse Disorder Action Plan. This four-part strategy studies several components, such as honey bee production and health status, pesticide exposure, and bee stress and immunity levels.

Finally, the EPA is doing its part to cease CCD by conducting thorough evaluations of all pesticides. Additionally, bee toxicity data is examined and further testing occurs when necessary. The agency also mandated the use of bee protection language on labeling in order to avoid the use of pesticides that are harmful to bees.

The bees bred for beekeeping are usually docile and gentle. They are happy to provide their services as long as they are treated with respect. They are social insects, much like ants and termites. This means that they live in groups of thousands, all of whom work together as a specialized unit to gather food, care for their young, and perform other life-sustaining responsibilities. If they are somehow unable to rejoin their colony, they will die.

The bees get their nutrients from the protein in the pollen and their carbohydrates from the honey. They feed their young a special food product known as "bee bread." Bee bread is a mixture of pollen, nectar, and honey. If a particular larva is perceived to be a future queen, she will receive a special nutrient called royal jelly that is secreted from the hypopharyngeal glands in the heads of young workers. Though all bee larvae eat some portion of royal jelly, only future queens receive it as their sole food source.

Bees are fascinating creatures, not only because of their ability to make wax and honey, but also because of their lifestyle characteristics, and mannerisms. Bees cannot function as single organisms. They are unique in the animal kingdom and serve as a model for humans.

Bees are insects with a hard skeleton on the outside, called an exoskeleton. The scientific term is "chitinous exoskeleton," which has several movable plates of chitin overlapping each other. Over these chitin plates are coarse and branched hairs that help in pollen collection and the regulation of body temperature. Chitin is a polymer of glucose that can support a lot of weight. This material causes bees to shed their skins several times during the larva stages and also prevents the bees from growing once they reach their adult stage.

Their bodies are divided into three sections and have some degree of flexibility because of a narrow neck and waist between the main sections. The specific organs of drones, workers, and queens all vary slightly. *To learn the body parts of a honey bee, see Appendix A.*

Head

The honey bee's head is flat and triangular in shape. It contains the brain and sensory organs that control sight, smell, touch, and taste. A bee's brain is a collection of approximately 950,000 specialized neurons.

There are two antennae on the front of the head, called "feelers." They are used for smelling, tasting, and touching. The feelers are made up of a basal stalk called a "scrape" and a long piece called a "flagellum" that is divided into 12 segments.

Although the drone's antenna has 12 segments, it is shorter than the female's antenna. The antennae are controlled by four muscles with thousands of tiny sensors that relay messages and help bees identify water, flowers, colonies, and obstacles.

The mouth, which includes the mandibles, is a complex body part. The mandibles are located on both sides of the mouth. Bees use their mouth and mandibles to collect pollen, carry water or food, feed the larvae, and form wax. The mandibles are like claws. They can pinch, hold, and grind by moving side to side. The mandibular gland is located above the mandibles. In the queen, this serves an important purpose: Her gland secretes her "queen substance," which is a powerful pheromone used to communicate with her colony and maintain the social organization. In drones, this gland is almost completely reduced.

The labrum is a wide plate on the front of the mouth, directly above the mandibles. Below the mandibles are the maxillae. The labrum and the maxillae support the proboscis. The proboscis is inside the mouth. This amazing body part is like a retractable straw, formed when the front part of the mouth, the labrum, and the maxillae come together. When needed, the proboscis sucks up water, nectar, and honey with the use of a pump inside the bee's head. The pump also works in reverse to push food out to young bees.

There are two large compound eyes at the front of the head that allow the bee to see in normal conditions. The compound eyes are actually clusters of smaller eyes, each with their own nerve endings that lead to the brain. These compound eyes are able to see polarized and ultraviolet lights. The ocelli — three smaller eyes used to see inside the hive — are located on the top of the head. On drones, the larger wrap-around compound eyes practically over-shadow their ocelli.

Thorax

The thorax is the middle section of the bee and where the two pairs of wings and six legs are connected. It serves as the bee's chest and contains holes called spiracles. Spiracles are used for breathing and are found all along the thorax and abdomen. Each hole is attached to the bee's trachea, where air passes through the bee's body by its own pressure and movement. The thorax contains all the muscles and organs used for transportability.

The two pairs of wings are attached to each side of the bee's body. When at rest, they can fold down separately, but when in flight, the pairs on either side work together. The wings are controlled by muscles in the thorax. They

can angle and straighten for optimum flight and hovering capabilities. Top-to-bottom movement is conducted by muscles that do not touch the wings. Instead, they contract and distort the shape of the thorax.

The thorax contains the bee's six legs. Each leg has six main joints with taste sensors at the tips. Each pair of legs is slightly different. The front two have a special device for cleaning the antennae. The middle legs are used for walking and for packing pollen and propolis into the pollen bags, which are attached to the rear legs. The legs are covered in tiny hairs used as brushes to comb the body free of pollen. At the end of each leg is a claw-like foot that allows the bee to adhere to rough surfaces. At the base of the food, there is a pad that helps the foot adhere to glass or other smooth surfaces.

Abdomen

The abdomen is where the bee's internal organs — heart, stomach, wax and scent glands, intestines, and stingers — are stored. The reproductive organs are also there. The males do not have the modified egg-laying apparatus, called an ovipositor, which serves as the stinger in the female species.

Bees actually have two stomachs: the honey stomach and their true stomach. The honey stomach, called the "crop," holds the pollen and nectar. When foraging, bees return to the colony hive and regurgitate the nectar into cells. The pollen is digested in the true stomach, and once the food is digested, it is absorbed in the intestine. The digested food passes through the intestine into the rectum, where it will stay until it is passed during a cleansing flight.

The stinger is a safeguard for the hive and colony. The poison released from the stinger causes pain, redness, and swelling. Some people are allergic to the stings and may experience anaphylactic shock or death. These are severe reactions, but the most common is a body rash. The males, or drones, do not have a stinger and can be handled by the beekeeper.

When a bee uses its stinger on another bee, it can use it more than once, but if the bee uses its stinger on a human or animal, the stinger gets lodged in the skin and pulls out a large portion of the bee's organs, resulting in death.

Castes of Bees

While all bees may look alike, there are three different castes, or types: queen, drone, and worker. It is important for a beekeeper to be able to tell the three apart. Certain characteristics can help with in this daunting task. Female bees can be either queens or workers, and female larvae that received large quantities of royal jelly will result in a queen. Male bees are called drones.

Queen

Everything that happens in and near the colony is for the queen. Bees fly out to forage, but if kept away from the hive and the queen, they will die. The queen is essential to the entire colony. Without her, the rest of the colony would cease to exist. The queen should be evaluated by the beekeeper on each visit to the hive.

In a bee colony, there is only one queen, but it is estimated that in up to 20 percent of managed hives, there may be two or more queens. She comes into her "royal" duties soon after hatching. When a queen lays eggs inside the cells of the hive, the nutrient royal jelly is placed in each cell. If a queen bee is desired, chosen larvae will receive larger quantities of royal jelly as their only food source for the first four days of growth. This rapid, early feeding triggers the development of a queen, including the fully developed ovaries needed to lay eggs. As they begin to hatch, those that have been fed the larger quantity of royal jelly and become queens will attack the cells of impending competitors. If more than one queen hatches at the same time, there will be a fight to the death.

One way to distinguish the queen from other bees is by her size. A queen is about 2 to 3 centimeters in length and is the largest bee in the colony. Some queens perform better than others. Determining if your queen is better than another queen is fairly easy: It is all about how productive the hive is. A hive can produce a lot of wax and honey and prepare a large brood for the new season, or it can produce little to none and produce small broods or all drones.

The queen has two important jobs: laying eggs and secreting "queen substance." She excretes pheromones that give direction to the rest of the hive. These pheromones draw other bees to her as well as stimulate brood rearing, foraging, and comb building; spur worker bees to rear more female eggs as workers; repress the growth of the ovaries; and stabilize swarms. The "queen substances" that she secretes comprise a variety of different pheromonal scents and do an array of important jobs.

One of the most crucial pheromones the queen secretes is called the queen's mandibular pheromone, or QMP. It regulates social behavior in the hive and affects hive maintenance, swarming, and mating. Queen retinue pheromone, or QRP, is another important queen substance. It controls how other bees respond to the queen, plus it helps drones find a queen while in flight 200 feet away.

Inside the queen bee's abdomen are two groups of tubes with which she lays her eggs. Each group is known as an ovary. Each tube produces eggs. She lays more than 1,500 eggs per day in intervals of 30 to 45 seconds. As she travels from cell to cell inside the hive laying her eggs, the worker bees will take care of her every need. They do everything that her size renders her incapable of doing for herself, such as feeding her, combing her, and disposing of her waste. She will start laying eggs in the center of the hive and work her way in a zig-zag pattern, laying eggs in the cells that the worker bees have prepared.

While the queen does have a stinger, she seldom uses it. Her stinger is used primarily for killing rivals. At times, a queen from another hive will become disoriented and enter a strange hive. She may also use her stinger in an act of supercedure (removing an older queen from her colony).

Queens usually live two to three years. They can become a drone layer and produce unfertilized eggs that become drones. When the queen is ready to mate, she will take short flights around the hive, then mate with 20 or more drones. Her compound eyes have fewer eye cells than the workers or drones because the queen is not required to carry out many of the mundane hive chores. The queen is the only female bee with fully developed ovaries, which makes her able to lay fertilized eggs. Many beekeepers will kill and replace the queen every two years to keep the hive active and productive.

Replacing the queen is called requeening. Simply go online or pick up the phone, and you can buy a new queen from a mail order company. She will arrive in the mail in a shipping cage containing sugar candy. However, it is a good idea to let someone at your local post office know that you will be expecting a shipment. Spray the new queen and her box with a sugar syrup, then take a small nail and remove the cork from the end of the queen cage containing sugar candy. Place the queen's cage on the hive's bottom board, over the top bars, or between two frames. Be sure the screen is facing toward the bees so they can feed the queen during the introduction. By the time the worker bees eat through the sugar candy and release the queen, they will have become accustomed to her pheromones and will accept her into the colony.

Worker

Worker bees are female and make up the majority of the hive. They have underdeveloped ovaries and cannot lay fertile eggs. Worker bees can lay eggs in the absence of a queen, but the eggs will become drones. Workers do all of the foraging, brood rearing, honey producing, and other work for the hive. A worker bee's job changes as they mature. They live about six weeks during the most productive parts of the year but live longer during the winter months, when the hive is dormant.

When first hatched, a worker bee will perform "housework" inside the hive. Her first task is to clean the cell from which she was hatched. She also will clean other cells and prepare them for an egg. Worker bees remove dead bees and diseased larvae from the hive and take the carcasses as far away from the hive as possible. On occasion, mice and other small animal intruders will enter the hive, where the bees will sting it to death. Because a mouse is too big for bees to carry out of the hive, workers will cover it with a substance called propolis — a type of bee resin or glue.

Nurse bees

A nurse bee checks larvae about 1,500 times a day to feed and care for their needs. They feed each larva a mixture of pollen, honey, and royal jelly. At seven to 10 days, the worker bees will begin to attend to the queen. They feed and groom her, remove her waste, and assist with egg-laying. When the worker bees are 12 to 18 day old, they will begin to oversee the nectar that the foraging bees bring back to the hive. They take the nectar and add an enzyme to it as they deposit it in designated cells. Once a worker bee is past 12 days old, until about 18 days old, she will also take turns fanning the nectar to expedite the evaporation process and cure the honey. It is important to maintain a perfect temperature in the hive to achieve the best honey and allow for the healthy development of the brood. The workers will line the hive entrance and fan feverishly to push air into the hive and, with other workers fanning inside the hive, will drive the air further into its depths. The bees outside the hive also serve another purpose: Under the end of their abdomen is the Nasonov gland. This gland secretes a sweet scent into the air. It is intoxicating to other bees and serves as a welcome home for the foragers.

Guarding the hive

A small portion of bees are specialized in guarding the hive. They inspect all bees that enter the hive and are like CIA agents, constantly guarding the queen and the residents of their hive. If they find that a bee is foreign, they will release an alarm pheromone to the rest of the colony, and the troops will rally to stave off the invader. If an invader is loaded with pollen, the guard bees are less likely to mount an assault.

Worker bees can be divided into two varieties: summer and winter. Both are similar, but winter bees have several clusters of fat cells in their abdomen. This is due to the increased amount of pollen that winter bees consume in preparation for the season. Winter bees can live up to six months throughout the cold season.

Specialist and generalist workers

Worker bees can be divided into two other categories: specialist and generalist. Specialist bees have specialized their pollen preferences to specific flowers. When a bee specializes its pollen collection in this way, it emerges from the hive at the same time that the plant begins to flower. Squash and sunflowers are two plants that use the services of specialist bees for their pollination and survival. Squash plants open their flowers early in the morning and, simultaneously, the bees that specialize in this plant's flower leave the hive in search of the plant's pollen.

Although specialist bees specialize in particular flower species, generalist bees do not. Generalists visit a variety of plants and flowers when foraging for pollen. They also have longer lives and work seasons because their food sources are more varied throughout the year.

Drone

Any egg that the queen lays will hatch. Unfertilized eggs hatch and become male bees — drones — and have specific duties. Their main purpose is to mate with queens in midair. They fly strongly and quickly, despite their larger size, and will chase a queen several feet in the air to mate, after which he will die. Drones have the misfortune of being expendable should the hive run low on food. For example, if the winter runs long and food in the hive begins to run short, the colony will force out the drones. They can also be devoured before they ever hatch. As workers perform their daily nursery chores, if it becomes apparent that there are more drones than necessary, then the attending workers may destroy the unhatched drones.

Drones are produced in the spring when the hive is strong. The queen will lay drone eggs into cells that worker bees have made larger. They also protrude farther out of the cell than workers and must have a protective wax covering built over them. When the time comes for the drones to emerge from their cells, they must rely on their sisters to chew away the wax cap.

Drones are larger than worker bees and wider than the queen. The drone's compound eyes are large and wrap around its entire head. Drones get a bad rap because they simply eat and mate, have no pollen sacks, and cannot assist in hive duties, but in fact are vital to the survival of the species because they carry a crucial half of the bee's chromosomes. They also discourage inbreeding, in turn strengthening their hive.

A colony can have up to 500 drones. During swarming season, a colony may find itself without adult drones. If the colony is strong, there will be a stronger population of drones. Once winter arrives, most drones are removed from the hive or neglected until they die. According to beekeeping expert and author Howland Blackiston, there are no drones in hives all winter. Once the weather gets cooler and the mating season comes to a close, the workers do not want the drones around because of their need for food during the winter months. Although it may seem harsh by human standards, the drones are then systematically expelled from the hive. This is a death sentence because the honey bee, regardless of the caste, cannot survive without the colony.

Life Cycle

The life cycle of a bee is what entomologists call a complete metamorphosis. This means that the cycle begins with an egg, develops into a larva, then a pupa, then emerges as an adult — all in the span of about 21 days. All bees remain in the egg stage approximately three days. The chart below shows the different birth cycles of the queen, worker, and drone. *To learn about the life cycle of a honey bee, see Appendix B.*

Stages	Egg	Larva	Pupa	Adult (hatching)
Queen	3 days	8 days; cell is capped at 7.5 days	5 days	Hatch on day 16
Worker	3 days	9 days; cell is capped at 9 days	9 days	Hatch on day 21
Drone	3 days	9 days; cell is capped at 10 days	12 days	Hatch on day 24

Egg

The cycle begins as soon as the queen lays an egg. The eggs of the hive are called the brood. An egg is laid in each, of the cleaned and expertly prepared cells after the queen's personal inspection. The cells are of different sizes, and the size determines the egg she will place inside. Drone eggs are placed in larger cells and workers in smaller cells. She places the eggs standing in the center of the cell. The egg remains in this form for three days and hatches into a larva.

Larva

The larvae look like pieces of white rice. They eat, grow, and shed their skin multiple times before becoming a pupa. The worker bees on nurse duty will feed the larvae royal jelly at first, eventually switching to a mixture of pollen and nectar. When the larva has grown to 1,500 times its original size, the workers will seal the larva in the cell with a wax cap. At this point, the larva will spin a cocoon around its body.

Pupa

The larva is a pupa once the cap is placed on the cell and the cocoon is safely around the body. This is when the shape begins to form: The eyes begin to take shape and legs form; the wings take shape and colorization begins; and finally, the small hairs that cover the body are evident. At the end of the pupa cycle, the now-mature queen or worker bee will chew through the wax cap and emerge ready to work. The worker bees on nurse duty will help the drone chew through the wax cap.

THE BeeKeeper BUZZ

"New beekeepers always have scores of questions," said beekeeper Charles Parton. "One of the most frequently asked questions is how they can identify eggs. Bee eggs or larvae resemble tiny, white grains of rice. The best way to view the eggs is by looking at the frame with the sun at your back. Older frames, however, make the eggs easier to detect because they are usually darker."

Communication

The way bees communicate is one of the great mysteries of nature. There are several theories as to how and why bees communicate. Years of research prove that bees communicate to let others in their hive know where food is and where drones congregate for mating purposes.

Dance

The dance that bees use to communicate is called the "waggle," which usually consists of a small figure-eight motion. The bees actually perform two types of dances, depending on the location of the harvest. One dance is for a close field of pollen and the other for a field farther away. The inside of the hive is extremely dark, thus bees must communicate using non-visual techniques. The larger and more intricate the dance, the farther away the field and the more difficult it is to reach.

Pheromones

Pheromones are used in the odor plume theory. According to Adrian Wenner, bee researcher and proponent of the theory, the bees' dance does little to direct bees, but instead it is pheromones, secreted by the workers, that tell others where to find the nectar. Each bee uses pheromones to communicate to each other differently. The queen's pheromones tell the other bees that she is present and what work they should do. Her scent attracts drones for mating and controls the drone population inside the hive. Worker bees emit their pheromone fragrance at the hive entrance to guide foraging bees back. They also have an alarm pheromone that triggers the rest of the colony to take protective action if the hive is in danger. Even bees in the larva and pupa stages emit a fragrance that tells the worker nurse bees their age and feeding needs.

A bee's gland is an important part of how they communicate. When a bee raises its abdomen and points the tip down, it is able to expose the Nasonov gland. Once the gland is exposed, small puffs of the Nasonov pheromone are released. The scent is wafted farther out when the bees beat their wings. This is called "scenting" or "fanning" and is only done by worker bees. The Nasonov gland pheromone tells lost and foraging bees how to get home, and it keeps swarming colonies together as they search out a new home.

CASE STUDY: GETTING STARTED IS NEVER EASY

Ilse Ackermann
Beekeeper in California

During my first year of beekeeping, I probably experienced every problem imaginable.

Two of my most prevalent problems were ants and robbing.

My solution for combating ants was to build low tables (about knee-high) to place my hives on; then, I put the table legs in buckets of vegetable oil. This prevents the ants from marching up to the hives. Still, I have to constantly monitor plant growth around the hives because one blade of grass can be a bridge for the ants.

Robbing was also a problem early on probably because there was a wild hive close to my hives. Bees can become agitated when they are being robbed. What I did to stop that was throw a damp sheet over the hives; my bees were able to get in, but the sheet stopped the robbers.

It is vital that new beekeepers be able to identify their eggs. The best way to do this is by holding the frame up with the sun over your shoulder. The eggs will be difficult to spot at first because they are minuscule, but the key is to look for white/translucent circles.

Spring is generally the best time of year to begin beekeeping. This way, the bees have spring, summer, and fall to build up their food supplies to survive the winter. But do not expect honey that first summer. Your colony is growing, and they will need all the honey they do make in that first season for food during the winter.

It is important to always leave a little honey in the hive; never take it all. The bees need some of it to survive on during the winter months. I usually leave about a super full of honey, but here in California, that is generous. I do not give my bees sugar water or artificial food.

It is not always easy to tell which of the capped cells have honey and which have brood. One way to distinguish the two is by color. The capped honey cells will look like the color of honey and are scattered around the outer edges, while the brood is usually darker and will appear in the middle/bottom of frames.

When it comes to tools, I prefer a smoker, a hive tool, bee brush, and a veil and gloves. A bee repellent such as Bee Gone will come in handy when emptying out a super to retrieve honey.

The best way to guard against pest and disease is to be vigilant. Be a responsible beekeeper, take note of everything that affects your colony, and be prepared to nip problems in the bud as soon as they arise.

Bee stings are inevitable, but I do not like stings, so I always wear gear. Last year, my husband helped me with my hives, and he was not wearing a suit. We had to go to the emergency room with 25 stings. I am not allergic, but I keep an EpiPen® on hand at all times in case someone else is.

Hive Life

The phrase "busy as a bee" is an apt description. Almost all the work is done by the worker bees, but even the drones have specific duties. The first activity the bees are introduced to in the hive is comb building. Workers begin to secrete wax chips from glands on the underside of the abdomen. The chips come out in small, white, sheet-like secretions. Beginning beekeepers might mistake the production of wax as a disease when they see the small, white flakes. The comb is the entire group of cells that the bees use to store their honey, pollen, nectar, and water. It is also used to hold their young as they metamorphose from egg, pupa, and larva to finally emerge as an adult bee.

In the winter months, bees will cluster together in a tight ball with the queen at the center. The tighter the cluster, the more body heat is retained and the better the chances are of the colony surviving the winter. Conserving body heat also saves on the amount of food eaten throughout the winter. At the beginning of the year, the queen will begin to lay eggs in the center of the hive. This is a hard time for bees because brood production requires food that is often at a dangerously low supply. In early spring, there are lots of new broods, but room in the hive is scarce. This is usually when swarming takes place. In late summer, the bees become insistent upon storing honey, pollen, water, and their own mixtures of bee food. Bees lay their eggs under these stored foods as insulation, and over the winter months they slowly consume them, moving up the hive as they do.

To keep the hive running efficiently, a number of chores must be done constantly. A worker bee will use the pheromone scents from the queen and the area around her to instinctively know what to do, and in what order. Housekeeping is an important part of hive life. Bees constantly clean their cells and use a special substance called propolis as a disinfectant. They spread a thin layer throughout the hive but also use it in larger quantities to seal cracks and large holes in the hive, as well as to cover dead animals and other potential hive threats. Propolis is another valuable substance made by bees because it is soft and pliable but dries to a hard substance that is impossible to remove completely.

All undertaking chores are performed by the workers and include disposal of dead colony members and diseased brood. They will also mummify dead mice, shrews, and anything that is too heavy to pick up and carry out of the hive. Many of the young worker bees take on the chores of nursemaid. These young nurses take care of the brood. Tending to the queen is another significant part of hive life. The queen gets her own royal court to feed her and help dispose of her waste. Some of these workers in the royal court also play the part of an OB-GYN nurse and encourage the queen while she is laying eggs.

Foraging is another hive "must-do." This task is saved for the older, more mature workers. Their first foray out of the hive consists of hovering near the entrance and darting about. They circle the hive in order to commit the location to memory. They also take special notice of landmarks to later help them navigate their way home. Foraging is dangerous for many reasons. Staying out after dusk can disorientate the bees so they cannot find their way back to the hive, and if the temperature drops too low, they can die before ever returning home. Other dangers come from birds and other insect; plus, the long flights are tiring and full of obstacles. Older workers that have been foraging for a few days will be darker and have tattered wings.

Fanning is another activity that happens throughout the hive. When standing near the hive during this activity, it sounds similar to a mini jet revving its engines. Bees fan their wings rapidly to regulate the temperature inside the hive and to help evaporate the water in the honey. Bees also fan to release the pheromone from their Nasonov gland, which tells returning foragers they are home, as previously mentioned.

Mating

Honey bee queens are not monogamous. In fact, they mate with dozens of drones at a time and preserve the sperm for the remainder of their lives. Research shows that this conduct results in a heritably assorted brood, which has been shown to be more productive and resilient than their genetically homogeneous insect cousins. A queen can be killed by her colony if she is perceived to have not mated with as many drones as a competing queen. Queens that mate with multiple drones have pheromones with a more calming scent, which makes them better able to control the colony.

Honey bees mate with drones from other colonies in mid-flight to prevent inbreeding. When a new queen reaches a certain age, then sometime soon past the 23rd day, she will wait for a warm, sunny day and set out to a drone congregation area — an area usually outside of small trees that have dense leaves. The honey bee will mate repeatedly here. If the congregation is heavy, she may return for consecutive days to become fully mated, but her mating is typically done on her maiden flight. The queen stores the sperm in a spermatheca and will disperse it throughout her life. In queen bees, the spermatheca is an important part of the female reproductive system: It is the storage place for the sperm and is where fertilization takes place.

Beekeepers can look at the spermatheca and tell if sperm has been received.

It is important to the colonies' survival that the queen find a day suitable to take the mating flight. Should it rain for several days and the queen not find a day to leave, she will never be fertile. Unfertilized queens only lay drones, in essence killing the colony because they cannot lay fertilized females to raise as their replacements.

Because honey bees always mate mid-air — away from the nest and high enough off the ground to be out of sight — most beekeepers know little about the mating process. What we do know is that on days with good weather, drone bees leave the nest and fly to certain areas, where they congregate in the air to wait for queen bees. When a queen flies into the area, the drones will chase her and, if successful, many of them will mate with her. Her mating flight is a very vulnerable period because of danger from predators and changes in weather conditions. So a special area nearby, where she can mate with enough drones in as short a time as possible, increases her chances of survival. It is very important that drones from many different colonies congregate together to help ensure a varied genetic mix for the queen to avoid inbreeding.

Foraging

We have already discussed worker bees and the fact that they have many jobs. One of these jobs is to forage, which is when a worker bee leaves the hive in search of food,

water, and other necessities. Workers do not begin foraging until their life is half over. Worker bees begin foraging
by facing the hive and darting around it in what looks to be
a haphazard fashion. This movement is actually the technique the workers use to memorize the look and smell of
the hive. After their initial "dart and dive" movement, they
will begin to orbit the hive in circles that get larger with
each flight pattern.

Bees have been dependent on flowers for millions of years,
and plants have perfected their features to attract all kinds
of insects that transport their pollen to other plants. Social
bees change flower species when collecting pollen, while a
solitary bee prefers a specific species. The bees that visit
one specific species are known as "monolectic;" they search
for plants that bloom at a certain time of year. "Oligolectic"
bees travel to a few different varieties and are most likely
found in temperate regions. Bees that travel to a variety of
flowers are "polylectic."

Foraging bees have to determine how far they should travel
for their food source. If a large source is far away, the bee
would use too much energy. Bees typically fly as far as
necessary for food, but when the weather and temperature
cooperate, a bee can visit up to 40 plants per minute. Optimal temperatures are between 60 and 89°F. Mature bees
have been known to travel as far as eight miles, but a typical search is about two to three miles from the hive. Bee
may make as many as five to 15 trips a day, while a water
collector can make more than a hundred.

The period when bees forage and gather nectar for the colony is called "nectar flow." This is a time when there is so much nectar production that the bees have more than the colony's immediate needs. This is converted into honey and stored in combs.

When foraging bees return, they are greeted by house bees that relieve them of their nectar and deposit it in the cells that have been prepared. Pollen, nectar, water, and eggs all have specific cells. When the nectar is deposited into the cells, the house bees add a special enzyme that causes the nectar to turn into honey. After the enzyme is added, the workers take turns fanning the cells to evaporate water and accelerate the honey-ripening process. Foraging bees in a mature hive will return at a rate of one per second or greater.

Swarming

Swarming is referred to as the division between beehives, which is done in a natural manner. These swarms usually result when a honey bee colony grows too large. As the hive continues to grow, and the number of worker bees exceeds the capacity of the hive, the bees in the colony will raise another queen bee, which will travel to a new location and form a new hive with about half of the workers and drone bees from the original hive.

Although overcrowding is typically the reason why swarming occurs, an older queen and a mild winter may also add to the swarming impulse. A swarm generally includes the old queen and about 50 percent of the worker bees in the hive, said Lynda Cook Rizzardi, president of the Knox County Tennessee Beekeepers Association. The worker bees from the swarming hive will follow the queen's scent and swarm. Each hive of bees has only one queen at a time. If the queen happens to leave or be pushed from the hive, worker bees from her hive will follow her scent and go wherever their queen mother goes, Cook Rizzardi said.

Bee populations tend to increase in late spring and early summer. At the beginning of the growing season, when there is plenty of food available and a large brood, the colony can become overpopulated and begin to swarm to find a place to live. A swarm may comprise 1,500 to 30,000 bees, including workers, drones, and a queen. Swarming is a part of the yearly life cycle of a honey bee colony and allows the colony to reproduce itself.

The main reason bees look for a new home is to secure the survival of the original colony. The bees must first prepare large queen cells. This is done by first preparing large queen cells to house a new queen. Several workers will stop their foraging and hive duties to search for adequate living conditions. This is called scouting. The existing queen, workers, and several drones will all leave the hive together. The bees that are left behind conduct business as usual and wait for the queen to emerge.

The bees that have flown from the hive will land close by and wait for the scouting bees to return. The scouts will find trees, bushes, or other convenient locations for a new home. Once they find a suitable location, they perform the communication dance to tell the other bees their location. Bees seldom build their combs in the open, but if there are no other means to protect their combs, they will build wherever they can. However, they prefer a hollow tree, an empty building, or the underside of a porch. The queen will begin to lay eggs, and the workers and drones will begin foraging and housekeeping duties.

A large swarm of bees can be frightening, but honey bees only defend themselves around their nest, their young, and their food supply. A swarm will not be on the defense unless they are provoked. As long as their combs are not interfering with human activity, they should be left alone. If the bees do find their way into a home, they can be removed or, if absolutely necessary, killed. In order to prevent a future swarm, the entry space should be contained with caulk or insulation.

It is not easy to determine if bees are beginning to swarm. New beekeepers often confuse bees that are simply cooling off with those that are about to swarm. It is an easy mistake; the temperature inside a hive can be unbearable, depending on the outside temperature. As an early beekeeping expert of the 1700s, Francis Huber concluded that hives could reach temperatures up to 93°F in January. Other beekeeping experts observed in the 1800s that temperatures inside the hives could get as hot as 105.4°, as recorded by zoologist Morten Thrane Brünnich.

In situations of intense heat, as previously described, huge clusters of bees will gather at the opening to the hive, sometimes for days, trying to escape the heat. They will often swirl their wings in an effort to cool the hive, which needs to remain at a temperature in the mid-90s to maintain a functional hive. That is the difference between swarming bees and bees just trying to cool off: Swarming bees will leave quickly; cooling bees will stay, or at least until the temperature inside the hive is more manageable. To help with the cooling, make sure there is adequate ventilation and water.

Bees may also gather at the hive opening and engage in a strange rocking movement. Believe it or not, the rocking motion is actually the bee's way of scrubbing and polishing the hive entrance and surface.

A swarm can sometimes be seen flying through the air like a big ball. This is an exceptional sight on a summer's day, said beekeeper Lynda Cook Rizzardi. Once the cluster of honey bees find a limb, hollow tree, empty hive body, or even an opening in a house, the bees will take up residence and begin making honeycombs and honey. Make sure the bees have perched some place accessible. Sometimes the bees will swarm in the uppermost branches of a tree or deep inside a bush. Though these situations make them more difficult to capture, it can be done. If possible, enlist the help of a family member or an adventurous friend. Try bribing them with a pot of delicious, fresh honey or new beeswax candles.

The next step is to gather the equipment. Get an empty super, or a large box and some honey. Make sure the super is large enough to accommodate the swarm. Wear a bee suit veil and gloves. Other supplies include a pair of pruning shears, a lopper, and a ladder, depending on where the swarm has clustered.

Take the super or box and place it directly under the hanging swarm. Remember that the entire swarm is clustered around the queen. It is important to capture the queen; if not, part of the swarm might die without her.

If the drop from where they are hanging into the box is a short one, just cut off the limb or whatever the cluster is hanging from. If that is not an option, shake it. Most of the bees will fall into the box and remain there once they find out there is honey in it. Be warned that shaking the cluster of swarming bees could mean losing the queen.

Once the majority of the swarm is in the super, close it and store in a cool, shady spot until dusk or early evening. Dump the bees into the hive or onto a white sheet in front of the hive. Another solution is to place the super into the hive.

Swarming, however, is not always a good thing. There are times when it is best to discourage swarming, especially if the hive is small and the larger half of the bees will be leaving. Fortunately, there are simple ways to discourage swarming.

One way to discourage swarming is to split the hive. Set up another brood box and honey super. Take four frames of brood (loaded with bees, but not the queen) and put them in the middle of the brood box along with six empty frames, three on either side. Make sure one or two frames have existing queen cells. Add two honeyed frames (also loaded with bees) in the middle of the new super, along with eight empty frames, four on either side. Before putting the top lid on, take two or three frames from your original hive and gently brush the bees into your new hive. Some of the bees will eventually return to the original hive, but most will stay. At this time, you may want to queen the hive, or you can wait for nature to take its course and let the new colony create its own queen. If you are going to queen the hive on your own, follow these steps:

1. Order a new queen from a mail order company, which will arrive in a shipping cage with sugar candy.

2. Find the old queen in your hive. Remove and destroy her.

3. Spray the new queen and the box she came in with the sugar syrup.

4. Use a nail to remove the end of the queen's cage.

5. Place the queen's cage on the bottom board of your hive. You can also place this on top of the hive's bars or between two of the hive frames.

6. Make sure the screen opens toward the bees so they can feed the queen (they will eat the sugar candy that came with the queen).

7. Usually, by the time the sugar candy spray is gone, the queen has been accepted by the other bees in the hive.

Species

Only members of the genus *Apis* are true honey bees, although other genus members are considered honey bees. With the exception of the north and south polar regions, honey bees exist all over the world. They are capable of surviving weather extremes. More than 44 breeds of honey bees have been identified, but only a few are desirable for beekeeping. Some bees have poor swarming habits; others are excessively aggressive while protecting the hive; and some do not have adequate food storage characteristics.

Italian (Apis mellifera ligustica)

Italian honey bees are black or very dark brown with yellow stripes, except for the drones of the species, which are mostly yellow. The queens are also a gold color, but a bit more striking. They tend to be smaller, with shorter hair than that of some of their darker black or dark brown cousins. This subspecies of honey bee is better suited for warmer climates, as they are used to the moderate winters and prolonged summers.

This species produces young all year long, with larger broods in summer and warm climates. The constant brood-producing is a desirable beekeeping trait. Italian honey bees are also popular with beekeepers because of their moderate temperament when it comes to beekeeping maintenance. Other good characteristics are their tendency to produce a lot of honey, but they are spare with propolis. The large broods work great for beekeepers who also use their bees to pollinate crops.

This breed is the most widely distributed of all the honey bees, but some of the traits that make them so desirable also make them undesirable. The large broods are known to consume much more food during the winter months, and they do not have good clustering skills. This causes them to leave small gaps between their bodies all winter, and this results in a loss of body heat. This is another reason extra food is consumed in the winter. All of this adds up to the possibility that a whole colony could be wiped out during a cold spell.

Italians honey bees are excellent housekeepers, and some scientists believe that this is a big factor in why the bees have a high tolerance for some diseases and pests.

Caucasian (Apis mellifera caucasica)

Caucasians bees are dark gray with light gray stripes. They are mild-tempered, easy to work with, and raise strong colonies that reach full strength in the mid-summer months.

These bees are not suited for areas that reach full nectar flow in spring, as Caucasian bees are prone to Nosema disease and pests. They use excessive propolis, making hive opening and closing difficult; they also swarm late in spring, if at all, and build slowly. Caucasian bees are known to rob and drift in spring and fall, when nectar flow is slow.

Of all the bee species, Caucasians have the longest tongues. This makes them valuable in the pollination process. They will also forage in less-than-perfect temperatures, which is a favorable trait because it keeps the hive happy and active in cold, wet climates. Holistic and natural health care providers are fond of Caucasian bees because of their high propolis production.

Carniolan (Apis mellifera carnica)

Carniolan bees are dark gray, even black, with gray stripes. Originating in Slovenia, these bees are used to cold winters and fast-changing weather conditions. They are quick to build and swarm in the summer, but slow down considerably in the winter months. Carniolans are the most mild-tempered and gentle bees of all.

The Carniolans tolerate all beekeeping maintenance, making them the second-most popular bee in beekeeping. They fight pests, yet maintain a gentle nature around beekeepers. They keep their population at the same level as their food supply, and they are masters at regulating egg production with seasonal changes.

This species is resistant to many brood diseases and to certain pests. They forage in early morning and late evening, use small amounts of propolis, and are prone to swarming.

Western European (Apis mellifera)

Western European bees are the newest thing in beekeeping. They resemble the Carniolan honey bees, are gentle and disease-resistant, and are high producers. They are gaining favor in the beekeeping industry primarily because of one important characteristic — mite resistance.

They use less propolis than typical Italian honey bees and show exceptional winter hardiness, hibernating in small clusters. They produce a high nectar haul per bee, build queen cells throughout the brood season, and may have a higher tendency to swarm.

African (Apis mellifera scutellata)

Africanized, or African, honey bees (AHB) are not commercially available and are not considered useful for beekeeping as a hobby. Regardless of what you may read in the papers, Africanized honey bees do not fly around in angry swarms and randomly attack people. With a wingspan that is usually less than 9 millimeters, however, these honey bees are usually very aggressive, and they become highly defensive when protecting their home. The irony in that, however, lies in the fact that their home can be just about anywhere. They tend to favor small areas. Some common nesting spots include water meter boxes, utility poles, house eaves, old tires, holes in the ground, and tree limbs; the list is almost endless.

The main problem with the Africanized honey bee is its extreme protectiveness of the hive and brood. Their area of protectiveness is ten times larger than the European honey bee, ranging up to 40 yards away from their nest. Commonly referred to as "the killer bees," once disturbed, these bees are relentless and will chase an intruder as far as a quarter of a mile before giving up and going home. A joke among beekeepers is they are well-named, because an *Apis mellifera scutellata* will definitely cause you to "scoot-a-lotta" — and fast.

African honey bees are hardy and very productive honey-makers, but their home bears a similar climate to South America, which is another reason why they are not very useful for beekeeping. They were imported from Africa to Brazil in 1956 for cross-breeding with the European honey bees that were not faring well in the tropics. The breeders thought the blending would produce a more temperate African honey bee, but they did not get the results they were looking for; the bees still maintained their aggressive behavior. This may have happened sooner or later, but sooner it was. This new hybrid escaped from Brazil in 1957 and began its migration up to North America to eventually cross over the Texas border in 1990. Since then, the African honey bees have been moving steadily across the southern United States, from California to Florida. It is too late to stop their migration; however, researchers are hopeful they will find a way to breed the aggressiveness out of the African honey bee.

Other honey bees

Buckfast

Buckfast bees were named for their birthplace, Buckfast Abbey, England, where renowned apiarist Brother Adam, a Benedictine Monk, developed the strain. The Buckfast bee is a hybrid bred to be genetically resistant to tracheal mites. Though Buckfast bees excel at brood rearing, they are prone to robbing and absconding with honey.

Starline

The Starline bee is an Italian hybrid and is sometimes referred to as the clover bee. It is a strain of the Italian bee and is the only Italian strain commercially available. They are mildly aggressive but highly productive in pollination. They do not winter well because of overcrowding and must be requeened annually.

Midnight

The midnight bee is a hybrid of the Caucasian and Carniolan. They are mildly aggressive and use tons of propolis, but winter extremely well in the northern United States.

Only the Western European honey bee (*Apis mellifera*) and the Eastern honey bee (*Apis cerana*) are kept in man-made hives. For years, man killed and plundered bee colonies to get their honey and wax, but through the years we have developed efficient ways to work with honey bees instead of against them.

Knowing the potential pitfalls and having an action plan are important first steps. Begin with a specific area's natural characteristics and progress to city, county, and state issues. Each is equally important and can stop potential beekeepers in their tracks if all the proper channels are not followed.

Getting Started

Once the decision has been made to become a beekeeper, there are many crucial factors to consider. The first is choosing the best time of year.

THE Beekeeper BUZZ

"The best time of year to begin beekeeping really depends on where you live, but spring is best," said Ilse Ackermann, a veteran California beekeeper. "This way, the bees have spring, summer, and fall to build up their stores to survive the winter."

For best results, plan to have all your hives built and bees ordered in time for an early spring arrival. Preparing for the bees ahead of time is not only smart for the bees' survival, but it makes the steps run smoother for you as the beekeeper. Following the natural course of a bee's life will make for the easiest beekeeping process.

Another important consideration is the location of the apiary. If the apiary is located in a private backyard, there are several factors to consider: Will there be nectar- and pollen-producing, flowering plants nearby? Is the site private and away from neighbors? And will there be shade and wind protection? From low spots in the yard to overexposure, there are a number of details that can make a difference.

CASE STUDY: BEEKEEPING 101

Ed Colby
Writer and Beekeeper

Before starting beekeeping as a hobby or career, check with your local agriculture department. Some states might require a special license or permit.

Some of the problems that can occur in the first year of beekeeping include poorly mated queens (they do not lay enough eggs), diseases, parasites, and spring frosts that kill flowers. Spring, when the hives are building in population, is the best time to begin beekeeping. It is important to begin the prep work any time during the year, but spring is the best time to install the bees and begin maintenance.

Three of the most frequently asked questions by new beekeepers are: what do the eggs look like; how much honey should be left for bees to survive during the winter; and how long can bees survive on the sugar water?

The answers to these questions are fairly straightforward, but other questions that have to do with disease prevention are not. Once a beekeeper has a situation occur with disease and pests, he or she searches for a way to prevent any and all diseases. Quite simply, there is no sure-fire way to keep disease and pests away. It is a constant battle.

For the new beekeeper, detecting eggs can be tricky. They look like miniscule grains of rice. They are hard to see, but once you get the hang of it, you can find them easily. Honey is valuable, and here in Colorado, I try to leave a couple of mostly full-brood supers to get them through the winter. It can be hard for newbies to tell which cells have honey and which have brood; again, it takes a little practice. One rule of thumb is that brood cells are convex. Helping your colony survive the winter is an important part of maintenance, and bees generally do well on sugar water. The amount of time they need will depend on the duration of your winters.

My hive tool — which I use to pry open honey supers, bee frames, and lids — is my most valued tool. It is essential, and every serious beekeeper needs one. As for using protective gear, I always wear a veil. I only wear gloves when the girls are agitated, and if they are really in a mood, which is rare, I don a bee suit.

One of the biggest mistakes a new beekeeper can make is worrying too much about the little darlings. They live and die in spite of all we do for them and to them.

Ed Colby writes a humor and human-interest column for Bee Culture *magazine. He has been a beekeeper since 1995 with more than 60 hives. He sells honey and pollen, and rents bees for orchard pollination. He got his start as a beekeeper because he wanted to have reliable pollinators for his sweet cherry orchards.*

Equipment and Cost

Beekeepers need specific equipment and tools, which can be expensive. Used equipment is not recommended, so expect to spend a few hundred dollars in the beginning. The more elaborate the equipment, the more expensive the start-up fees.

Basic costs

The start-up costs for a new beekeeper will depend on the size of the operation. The basic equipment for just one hive will cost $150 to $300. A package of bees — which numbers about 3,000 — and a queen cost $65 to $70. The equipment to extract the honey varies. The cost of an uncapping knife, a tub for uncapping, a storage tank, and a strainer is about $100. The expense is in the honey extractor, which can cost $250 to thousands of dollars. It is best to hold off on the purchase of a honey extractor until the decision has been made to stay in the beekeeping business. For the beginner, with just one or two hives, there will be local beekeeping association groups that are usually willing to loan their equipment and even help with the first extraction.

Hive

The beehive is more than a box full of bees. It is the bees' home and must be built to specification, if they are to be as

productive as possible. The beekeeping boxes that are purchased or made are meant to impersonate the bees' natural hive. The boxes are made of several sections to give the
bees ample room to work and live, as well as give the beekeeper room to maintain the hive adequately.

At one time, man made hives were primarily "fixed frame,"
and in order to remove the honey, the comb had to be
destroyed. "Movable frames" are popular now and allow for
the removal of layers of the hive and the honey without
destroying the hive and comb.

Traditionally there have been three types of hives: tile, skeps,
and bee gums. Tile allowed the bees to thrive in baked-
clay tiles. Skeps were grasses or reeds woven together in a
single-section container. To harvest the honey, the skeps
were squeezed until honey dropped out, and later the bees
were destroyed. Gums were constructed from hollow trees
— often the red gum tree. This type also required eradica-
tion of the colony to extract the honey.

Modern hives have the bees' natural tendencies in mind
and work in conjunction with their innate habits and
movements. There are two types widely used today, and
both are movable frames: the Langstroth and other top-
bar hives, and leaf hives (which open and are worked from
the back). Langstroth hives and those similar to it can be
placed anywhere. They can be in an apiary, in a neighborhood, or in a farm field. Leaf hives are kept inside a bee
house. Because of the need for a bee house, Leaf Hives are
not popular choices among beginning beekeepers.

Rev. Lorenzo Lorraine Langstroth invented the movable frame hives. He introduced and patented his design in 1852, and it is now used by more than 75 percent of beekeepers in the world. Over the years, modifications have been made, such as changes in the size and number of layers, but it is the same basic idea designed by Langstroth. This type of hive was also instrumental in cutting back on the use of propolis by bees. Langstroth incorporated the discovery of "bee space" into his design. The bee space is the observation that bees cover spaces less than ¼ inch — such as between boards — with propolis, and they will fill larger spaces with wax.

Top-bar hives are similar in structure, but are built more simply. They are used by some people in the United States but are most often found in developing countries. They have top bars, no sides, or bottom. There is no foundation for the bees to build their comb upon. Instead, the bees build the comb so that it hangs from the top bar. Bees are encouraged to raise their brood in a separate part of the hive so that honey can be extracted without loss of bees.

The basic, movable frame hive consists of about seven sections. The outer portion of the hive, which is most visible to onlookers, is the hive outer cover, which provides protection from the adverse weather conditions.

Just inside the outer cover is the inner cover. It is necessary for insulation, but also to prevent bees from building a comb directly to the outer cover. At the top of the beehive, inside the inner and outer covers, are the honey supers.

This is where the bees store their honey surpluses and where they are harvested. Each box, or "super," is filled with 10 frames. The bees fill the frames with comb and honey, and the honey they use to live off is stored elsewhere. Feeders are usually attached to the top of these supers. Feeders provide food for the bees when the nectar flow is low, such as during the fall and winter months.

In many beehives, there will be a queen extruder as a divider. It keeps the queen in the brood box so that she will not lay eggs in the honey supers. This does not usually happen, however, and is not even necessary if there are two hive bodies. The queen extruder is a piece of wood that is placed between the honey super and the brood box or hive body. The workers can squeeze through, but the queen is too big.

Hive bodies are the boxes in the hive that contain most of the excitement. They are deep supers that have ten frames inside with foundations for the bees to build their comb. This is where the bees raise their brood and store the honey for their own use. One hive body will serve a colony well, but those in colder climates with rougher winters often use two.

The bottom board is just that: the bottom of the hive. It rests on the hive stand, which has a sloped landing pad that makes it easy for the bees to land and walk into the hive.

Frames and foundation are also needed for the hive. The frames are the thin, wooden pieces that fit into each super in the hive. They have sheets of foundation that serve as a starter kit for the bees to begin building their comb. The foundation has prefabricated hexagonal shapes that the bees use to guide them when making the wax cells for the comb. Most bee suppliers coat these foundations with a thin layer of wax so the bees will not have to expend too much energy getting started.

Movable frame hives

There are many advantages to using movable frame hives. The first advantage is that it eliminates the need for a bee house; second, it offers the ability to adjust the number of supers and brood boxes in the hive; and third, it allows nucleus colonies to form by using a queen extruder when adding more supers.

Photograph provided by FDACS-DPI (University of Florida)

Colonies in a movable frame hive grow stronger and produce more honey. The most notable disadvantage of movable frame hives is the weight.

Leaf hives

Leaf hives have frames that are removed from the back of
the hive. The back opens like a large hinged door, and the
frames sit inside vertically. There are two sections of the
vertical frames or leaves, which are divided by a metal grid.
The brood frames are above the grid, and the honey frames
are below. Worker bees can easily pass through the metal
grid to work the entire hive, but the queen bee is too large
and stays in the brood nest. The frames are covered with a
wooden frame containing a glass window.

Leaf hives are not without their certain advantages as
well. One great advantage is that they are excellent space
savers. They can be stacked on top of each other in bee
houses; they can be worked while sitting down. This
allows older or handicapped beekeepers to enjoy their
hobby more comfortably.

The biggest disadvantage of the leaf hives is that they must
be inside a bee house. A bee house is a structure that is
large enough to contain the hives and the beekeeper while
he or she works the hives. The house offers convenience
and protection from the weather; it hold the hives, the tools,
and equipment you use to keep the bees. It can also have
a separate workroom and honey extraction room. Bees are
a bit more trouble to handle in this type of hive because

they can fall off into a tray. The tray, however, can ease the bee's entry back into the hive, and thus is a necessary tool for this type of hive.

Smoker

Beekeeping without a smoker is a tedious experience. The main purpose of a smoker is to confuse the bees and make communication among them difficult. Like most other insects, bees will become frightened at the first signs of fire. As smoke is puffed into the hive, the bees deep inside the hive begin to stuff themselves with honey in preparation of impeding flight, should fire engulf the hive. The bees become so preoccupied by the threat of fire that they are no longer concerned about intruders. The bees at the entrance will frantically give off their warning pheromone, but the smoke will disguise the scent and prevent it from spreading to the other bees.

Light your smoker by inserting a loosely crumpled piece of newspaper. Once lit, use the bellows to stoke the flame enough to catch a few small pieces of wood chips. When the flame is stronger, add larger wood chips. Another great fuel source are cow chips; they burn long and hardily. Certain fuels like pine straw, burlap, and grass tend to smoke better than others.

Do not lift the top without first covering the closed hive with smoke. The smoke will seep into the cracks and crevices of the hive and begin to affect the bees. When the hive is open, continue to smoke the bees, then put the smoker nearby so that the smoke wafts throughout the hive. Pay attention to the color, feel, and density of the smoke that emanates from the smoker. It should be a cool, white puff, thick and cloud-like.

THE BeeKeeper BUZZ

"The smoker is my best friend," said Howland Blackiston, beekeeping expert and author. "Smoke calms the bees and allows for safe inspection of the hives. The smoker is a fire chamber with bellows designed to produce lots of smoke. Learn how to light it so that it stays lit, and never overdo the smoking process — a little smoke goes a long way."

Smokers are also used to herd bees in a certain direction. Pay attention to the direction the wind is blowing when your intention is to get the bees to move from one place to the other. Just the right amount of smoke should be used to encourage movement. Bees must have a clear sense of where they can go for a fresh breath. If there is too much smoke, this will cause the bees to become disoriented and unable to find the smoke-free areas.

A general-purpose smoker is approximately 4 by 7 inches. It should have a hook connected to the bellows so that it can be attached to a belt. A seasoned smoker is easier to light than one that has never been lit. Do not clean or scrape tar from the smoker until it affects the weight and use.

When not in use, keep the smoker and the fuel in a water-tight box in a cool, dry place, and keep a fire extinguisher handy. A fire extinguisher should always be kept near when fire of any type is in use.

Feeders

There are a variety of feeders on the market. They vary in levels of simplicity, and some can be made at home. The simplest type of bee feeder can be made from a pickle jar with holes poked in the lid.

Fill the jar with sugar-water syrup and replace the lid tightly. When the jar is turned over, just a few drops should appear, then the flow should stop. Take two thin pieces of wood to the hive and place them over the feeding slot; place the upside-down jar on top. Cover the feeder with an empty brood box or super and place the lid back on the hive. A small jar with the sugary syrup inside must be refilled every day. If your colony is strong, it can easily drain a small feeder in a day.

There are also round feeders, such as the Miller or the Ashforth. Bees enter from the bottom to get at the food. Using a round feeder requires a small amount of modification to the hive: A small-hive box should be placed around it to deter robber bees and other unwanted visitors. One caution for these types of feeders is that because they are made of wood, some insects, like wasps, will attempt to chew through the wood to get to the food syrup inside.

Begin feeding at night after the bees have returned home. Placing the feeder inside at night allows the bee to communicate with each other about the food source. After the initial feeding, the feeder can be refilled any time. Start feeding in late summer and continue for as long as necessary. This will depend on the types of plants that bloom throughout the winter.

Making bee candy is a fairly simple process. Heat half a gallon of water; gradually add a ½-pound of sugar; mix until the sugar begins to boil; let the mixture boil rapidly for about three minutes. Place the pan in a tub of cold water and let stand while continuing to stir until the mixture cools. Once the mixture begins to get cloudy, pour into small molds or into a large metal dish. Keep the molds in plastic bags in a cool, dry area until ready to use.

Hive tool

A hive tool is generally used for opening the hive and for removing propolis. This tool is absolutely indispensable for beekeepers.

Bee brush

A bee brush is used to gently brush bees off the hive when inspecting the frames. A gloved hand, or a tree branch with leaves also works, but a brush is less invasive.

THE BeeKeeper BUZZ

"It is important to have all the proper tools and gear on hand before starting the installation," said beekeeper Charles Parton. "Be sure to include, a hive tool, smoker, bee suit, gloves, and veil. Novice beekeepers might find the gloves and a veil are especially useful, until they get accustomed to their hives and bees."

Clothing

A beekeeper should be conscious of his or her clothing. Not everyone wants to wear a bee suit, especially in the warmer climates; however, it is important to wear light colors and smooth textures. Bees are attracted to darker colors, especially black, blue, and red. Dark or heavy clothing such as wool can closely resemble a bear's fur or any other marauding animal, which cause the bees to use protective stings in defense of its hive. Layering light clothing is also another great way to protect against stings.

Bee suit and bee jacket

A bee suit is a comfortable and durable one-piece suit made from cotton or polyester, and it has tightly cuffed ankles and wrists that fit snugly into boots and gloves. Some also have an attached hood and veil, or a ventilated, protective helmet. As much protection as they provide, bee suits are not completely impenetrable; there is always one steadfast bee that will find a way under a flap or beneath a cuff. A bee jacket with a hood and veil is a nice compromise. Less constricting and cooler, the jacket is a small investment for the protection it provides.

All photographs on this page are provided by FDACS-DPI (University of Florida)

Hood and veil

The bee veil and hood are exceptionally helpful. Bees, especially when in alarm mode, are attracted to noses, eyes and mouths, and they have a tendency to get tangled in hair. Wearing a bee veil and hat provides protection for the face and neck. A hood with a veil can be purchased separately, but a complete bee suit is recommended.

Gloves

Gloves are another good investment for every beginning beekeeper. They provide protection for the hands and upper arms. The gloves are made out of soft, pliable leather and offer a fair amount of feeling through them. Many experienced beekeepers discontinue using their gloves after they become familiar with the temperament and actions of their bees.

Bees

A beekeeper needs bees, obviously. There are two ways to get bees into your hive: buying or capturing them. Capturing bees is an option but not recommended, especially for the new beekeeper. Before bees are purchased from one of the many available bee suppliers, it is important to assemble all the necessary equipment. Plan to order your bees so that they can arrive in early spring — sometime between February and April.

A new beekeeper should start with approximately 2,500 to 3,000 bees and a queen. They arrive in a wooden, screened package. There is some degree of stress and agitation to the bees in the transportation process, so there might be an inch or so of dead bees in the bottom of the package. This is normal because the older and weaker bees will die from temperature and feeding issues during the trip.

A package of bees can be stored for a few days before installation into the hive. Have everything in place so that installation can begin no later than three days after the bees' arrival. Any longer than three days is putting the colony at risk. When your package arrives, take a few precautionary steps to make sure that your bees remain alive during installation.

Bees increase their activity level when it is warm and sunny. Storing them in a cool, dry place keeps their activity to a minimum, saves their energy, and increases their chances of survival.

Keep them full by feeding them syrup, sugar water, or bee food. Although a can of sugar syrup is included in the shipment, not all the bees will have access to it. It is a good idea to spray the bees with a solution of sugar water every four to five hours.

Bees can be purchased from other beekeepers or through the mail. If you choose to buy your bees from another beekeeper, there are a few traits to look for before the purchase is complete, beginning with your observation of the bees. While observing them:

- Stand by the hive for a while and see how long it takes before they sense your presence. They should be used to a beekeeper and human company.

- Try to observe the bees on a sunny day. Make sure they are active and flying in and out of the hive entrance. This is an important sign of a healthy hive.

- The bees flying into the hive should also be laden with pollen. Ask the beekeeper to open the hive; this will provide some insight into the bees' temperament.

Author's Apiary

Joining beekeeping associations to learn more

There are three national beekeeping associations and 27 state beekeeping associations in the United States. Below the state level, the next groups are typically county or city associations; i.e. Alachua County Beekeepers Club (FL), Southwest Michigan Beekeepers Association, or Houston Beekeepers Association (TX). A great site to find a Bee Club in your area is **www.honeyo.com**.

What should you do if you cannot find a club nearby? You guessed it: Start your own. If you can find a group of people who are interested in bees and beekeeping and would like to meet regularly, you have a club; it could be that simple. Meet once a month, bring in speakers, talk about bees, and just have fun.

Take your time and decide if the group would like to take the next step and become a nonprofit (501c3) organization. There are advantages to doing this, and it gives you a mission base to help our honey bees. To find out more information on how to start an official nonprofit organization, go to **www.irs.gov/charities**.

Location, Location, Location

Choosing a location for your bees and hive is more than picking the spot by the rose bush. Bees should be placed close enough to pollen sources, but far enough from neighbors and homes to make everyone comfortable. If possible, hives should face southeast. Another option is to move your bees as seasons change, with a winter and a summer location.

Hive placement has a big impact on how much work must be done to keep your hive healthy. It also has a lot to do with how much honey and wax are produced. There are several factors to keep in mind when deciding the exact location for your hive:

- *Water and food:* A honey bee's average foraging flight is about 2 to 3 miles from the apiary. Hives should be placed no farther than 6 to 7 miles from flowers, plants, and crops.

- *Shade:* The hive should be in an area that is dappled with shade — not total shade, but not total sun.

- *Drainage:* There must be proper drainage for your bees to survive. Bees cannot survive in marshy or exceptionally wet conditions. There must be adequate runoff in rainy conditions and firm ground for your bees to thrive.

- *Air:* Put your hive in a place that gets cool breezes and good airflow. Air that remains stagnant is bad for your bees.

- *Accessibility:* Make sure that access to and from the hive and your entire apiary is convenient.

The flight habits of bees already in the area are another important aspect. Encourage flight patterns that take bees away from homes and children's play areas. If there is a large field of clover or a grove of flowering trees to the south of your home, take advantage of the traffic flow. Encourage bees to fly and forage in that direction by placing the hives strategically to face in that direction.

Beekeepers should factor in their home for this equation. This is known as the accessibility quotient. Most beekeepers prefer to place their hives close to their homes. It is convenient when it comes to maintenance, storage, and emergency situations.

While it is important that a hive has an appropriate amount of shade, it is equally as important that there be adequate sunlight. This is of special concern in the winter months — bees that are kept in the shade are usually more ill-tempered.

Vegetation surrounding the area is another deciding factor. Tall trees can be used as protection from winter winds and storms. The area should be easy to mow. Do not leave tall grasses or weeds around the hive, because this could hinder proper ventilation.

Once an appropriate location has been chosen, make sure the area is neat and clean. Consider installing a fence around the apiary if neighbors, children, or animals are a concern. Ants and other insects could also cause a problem for your bees, so treat the area with an insecticide before installing your bees.

Laws and Ordinances

Whether your decision is to have one hive or a dozen, it is imperative that all beekeepers understand all state and local laws. Before any monetary investments are made, check with your local officials on ordinances, permits, rules, and regulations.

In most places, it is legal to keep bees. In some communities, apiaries are considered a benefit to the community. Even if your community does not have laws against beekeeping, they might have a limit on the number of hives allowed in a neighborhood. Some states may also require an inspection from a state agency.

Check with your insurance company about insuring your apiary. Insurance companies will have different concerns about liability. The American Beekeepers Federation has a program for its members, but local clubs and organizations might have additional information.

Besides following the laws and ordinances for beekeeping and your apiary, you will also need to follow the laws for the sale and marketing of your bee products. This may mean manufacturing the products in a certain way, as well as obtaining certain specific permits and licenses.

CASE STUDY: MUST-KNOW ADVICE FOR EVERY BEEKEEPER

Lynda Cook Rizzardi
Beekeeper

Once a beekeeper decides to pursue beekeeping as a hobby or a business, it is important that he or she put in ample time to ensure healthy and productive hives of honey bees.

"In early spring, it is important to check the hives to be sure the bees have wintered well," said Cook Rizzardi. "In east Tennessee, our winters are generally not too cold for extended periods of time and often not harsh enough for healthy hives to freeze."

If the hive food stores are in short supply in early spring, feeding is recommended to ensure that the honey bee colony will be ready for the queen bee to begin laying eggs. A queen can lay 2,000 eggs or more a day — especially in the summer, when a heavy honey flow is on.

Bee space is very important. Most traditional hives are constructed of wood. Metal frame spacers can be nailed in the top of the hive body to maintain the proper ⅜-inch bee space. Bees have a tendency to build excess comb in wider spaces. If the bees have too much space, the beekeeper will find opening and working inside the hive body more difficult because comb is a very sticky, gooey substance.

The number of hive boxes/supers added depends upon the number of worker bees in the hive and the amount of honey nectar brought into the super to be placed in the comb cells. During a heavy flow, when plants and trees are blooming and there is an abundance of pollen and nectar, a beekeeper will continually add supers for the honey stores.

Honey bee swarms are common when there is not adequate space in the hive for all the worker bees and when there are frequent changes in the weather conditions. A swarm generally includes the old queen (sometimes a new queen) and about 50 percent of the worker bees in the hive; the worker bees from the swarming hive will follow the queen's scent and swarm. Each hive of bees has only one queen at a time. If the queen happens to leave or be pushed from the hive, worker bees from her hive will follow her scent and go wherever their queen mother goes.

A swarm can sometimes be seen flying through the air like a big ball. This is an exceptional sight on a summer's day. Once the cluster of honey bees find a limb, hollow tree, empty hive body, or even an opening in a house, the bees will take up residence and begin building honeycomb and making honey. If a beekeeper has a hive body that is excessively full of honey bees, he or she can split the colony by taking a double handful of bees and placing them in a newly prepared hive body with a few frames of brood, a few frames or honey, and a new queen bee. Requeening hives each year, in the spring or late summer, will generally prevent swarming and provide a productive queen bee for the hive.

Beehives are easier to maintain and to work in when placed on stands approximately 1 foot off the ground. Not only does this save the beekeeper's back when repeatedly bending over to work, but it helps to avoid skunks, which are particularly drawn to the hives and enjoy the sweet honey. Scratch marks on the front of a beehive is often evidence of the presence of skunks. Mice can also invade and take up residency in a weak hive, and when they need a warm home on cold days, they work their way into a hive and eat the honey. Sometimes the bees can attack and kill intruders, but the larger the intruder, the more difficult the task.

"The most disastrous experience that my father and I had with beehives was caused by a family of black bears," said Cook Rizzardi. "My father liked to move colonies around for different blooms (trees and flowers) to have a variety of flavors and colors of honey. One summer in the mountains, the bears found the beehives and really enjoyed smashing the wooden boxes to reach the honey inside. After cleaning up the mess and establishing a new area a few miles away, once again, the bears found the beehives. Luckily for us, we were not bothered or attacked while setting up the hives. We simply chose not to return to that area the next summer."

When moving honey bee colonies, try to move them at night, use straps to secure the hive body, and attach a screen cover with wooden end bars to the front entrance of the hive. Most all the bees will return by dusk, secure the hive, and move to their new home location. Honey bees have a keen sense of direction and will return to only their hive because each hive has a distinctive scent or aroma that the bees recognize. When an unfamiliar honey bee, other insect, or other intruder attempts to enter the hive, the guard bees quickly communicate the intrusion, and several worker bees will come to the entrance to help defend the hive.

Protecting the colony is now more difficult because of all the honey bee diseases, such as tracheal and varroa mites, small-hive beetles, American foulbrood, and nosema.

Be warned: All beekeepers generally get stung at some time. The queen and the worker bees have a stinger, but the drones (male bees) do not. Once a worker bee stings, the stinger leaves the little bee body behind, and the bee dies.

As a basic rule, a colony consists of a deep and a shallow, or two mediums, as a brood chamber, as well as a shallow super of honey for the honey bees. During the summer — when the beekeeper is adding supers for honey production — add one, two, or three at a time, depending upon the number of honey bees in the colony and the distance of the colony from your home. Try to check on the colony weekly; be sure to allow room for honey stores to prevent swarming.

Once the beekeeper harvests the capped, sealed, and stored honey, always leave a full super of honey for the bees to winter on. In the winter, the queen will generally remain in the lower brood box; therefore, the second brood box should also contain honey to help feed the bees. Most hives will need about 40 to 50 pounds of honey to survive one winter. On average, a shallow super of honey will weigh between 30 and 35 pounds; a medium super of honey will weigh between 40 and 45 pounds; and a deep super full of honey will weigh between 60 and 70 pounds.

The capped honey cells will be clear, smooth, and even across the top, and one can observe that there is honey inside the cell, whether the honey is light or dark in color. Honey inside cells has a glistening glow, and the frame of honey will be heavy when lifted from the super. Furthermore, the lighter the color, the thinner the honey and the milder the taste; the darker the color, the thicker the honey — and often times the more flavor in a single bite of honey. The brood cells will be slightly raised (for a worker bee), shaped like a peanut on top of several cells (for a queen), or shaped like a protruding bullet from the cell (for a drone). All the brood frames of wax are generally darker because of the eggs having been laid and hatched repeatedly in the same cells as they walk across the brood to travel higher in the hive body to deposit the honey.

Sugar water is a food source; therefore, the honey bees could live indefinitely on sugar water as long as the beekeeper is willing to always prepare the syrup, feed the bees, and check on the colony every few days. Some beekeepers who want to produce a thin, clear product to sell will simply feed the colony until the supers are full. The downside to this process is that because the honey bees have not gathered and processed pollen and nectar, the product is considered adulterated honey (fed sugar water), and will crystallize and look like the granulated sugar the bees were fed.

Special licensing:
If honey, wax or hive products are to be sold, it is important to label each product with the seller's name, address, and telephone number. For those beekeepers with much honey to process, a honey house or separate building is required for health and sanitation reasons. Do not use a house kitchen. If samples are to be distributed to the general public at a fair, craft, or vendor event, the county health department must issue a letter granting permission for distribution.

Honey bees are not often found in the wild very often because of the pesticides used in general sprayings around homes and businesses. Honey bee diseases have also been transmitted to wild bees that have tried to forage from a particular colony, then returned to their home with a disease that wiped out the wild hive as well.

Cook Rizzardi's experiences catching a wild hive:
"Some summers provide more opportunities for collecting swarms or a hive on the run. One of the most memorable for me was several years ago," said Cook Rizzardi. "My mother and I saw the swarm fly through our yard one afternoon to a small tree limb. My father and I collected an empty hive body, suited up, and visited our neighbor's yard. By the time we arrived, the bees had settled a little and were calmly humming and buzzing to let everyone know their presence.

"We placed our empty hive body on the ground. My father shook the limb twice, and the bees fell into the box with frames of comb. I placed the lid on the box, and we stepped back to watch. Most of the remaining bees quickly sensed they had a new home. We went home, but later that evening we drove back to the tree, loaded the beehive, and carefully drove home — mission accomplished."

Lynda Cook Rizzardi was the 2009 President of the Knox County Tennessee Beekeepers Association; member of the Knox County and Tennessee Beekeepers Associations; and secretary of the Tennessee Valley Honey Show for 12 years.

Her interest in beekeeping can be attributed to her parents. For many years, her father kept anywhere from three to 55 hives at one time. Her family grew up eating honey and learning about the life of honey bees. Cook Rizzardi enjoyed cooking and using honey and always had a variety of honeys to eat — her family would enter honey in the Tennessee Valley Fair in Knoxville, and she and her father won several ribbons and a few of the sweepstakes trophies. Her mother served as secretary of the Blount County Beekeepers Association for many years, as well.

Neighbors and Other Nuisances

Most beekeepers live in suburbs with plenty of flowers, but it is not uncommon to have hives on rooftops. Bees will travel for miles to find nectar and pollen, so the flowers do not have to be close by.

But be prepared: Not everyone will be as enthusiastic about your hobby as you are. When someone hears that their neighbor is a beekeeper, they might immediately dredge up scenarios of bee attacks, complete with huge, black clouds of swarming, angry bees.

Most of the animosity your neighbors might have is simply due to ignorance. Taking the time to educate your friends, family, and neighbors is a step in the right direction. Invite them over to watch a hive inspection; this is the best way to demonstrate how docile the bees are.

There are few things that can be done to minimize trouble from your neighbors. Have a fresh water supply for your thirsty bees. If you do not want the expense of a birdbath, place a few chicken waterers on a tree and set the hive close to it. If this does not persuade the bees to stay in their own backyard, try using sugar water. After a few days of using sweetened water, switch back to plain water and the bees will remain at home.

Paint or stain your hives a natural shade to blend in with the surroundings, or buy them already painted. Also, if your bees are in a residential neighborhood, restrict yourself to one or two hives. Bees fly up and away when they leave the hive; make sure they are well away from the entrance of your home.

Place your hive in a place that is inconspicuous. If your neighbors cannot see your hive, they could forget it is in your backyard.

Finally, give your neighbors, family, and friends gifts from the bounty of your hives. Jars of honey, candles, lotions, and other products make wonderful gifts when placed in a basket with a lovely bow. It goes a long way for keeping the peace among neighbors.

Author's Apiary

Have bees, will travel

Do not be discouraged if, after deciding you would like to be a beekeeper, you realize that due to area restrictions, crabby neighbors, or lack of space, you do not have a place for an apiary. There are options. You may have to do some more legwork, but it will be worth the effort. I have listed several ideas below to get you started; you may be surprised at the interest your inquiries will generate.

Thanks to all the publicity about our bees, people are more informed and, although they may not want to actually be a beekeeper, forming a partnership with one could be the next best thing. It is a win-win situation: Your honey bees can help the gardens, be a teaching tool to heighten community awareness, and perhaps even turn a profit for both you and your partner.

Consider the following options for creating an optimal location for you bee garden:

- Community garden
- Botanical garden
- Teaching farm
- Business rooftop
- Monastery
- Local farm
- Garden club
- Girl Scouts/Boy Scouts
- Non-profit organizations

Timing

Timing is important in beekeeping. Prepare your hive purchase or construction ahead of time. All laws and ordinances must be abided by, as well as any permits or registrations taken care of. Have the location scouted out and prepared.

CASE STUDY: ANSWERING THE QUESTIONS OF FIRST-TIME BEEKEEPERS

Jason Gropple
Beekeeper

First-time beekeepers often wonder about the problems they might encounter when they first start out. The answer is: anything and everything could and will go wrong — everything from smoker and equipment problems to weather, absconding, and starvation.

New beekeepers always ask about finding eggs. They are hard to detect, but in an active hive, they are most often seen in the center of the bottom of the cells. Hold the bee frame by the ears with the sun to your back, so the sunlight illuminates the cells. The eggs will show up more easily when the comb is dark from frequent use, but the new comb is almost the same color as the eggs — white.

December is the best time to get your hives ordered, put together, and painted; January is the time to order your bees. Depending on your climate, starting a new hive is best when the first round of dandelion blooms have begun to go to seed.

As winter approaches, it can be difficult to tell how much honey to leave for the bees to live on and how much can be taken. Those who live in cold climates should leave them more food. If your winters are warmer, leave your bees 25-30 pounds of honey (one shallow super above their brood. Of course, it is important to tell which capped cells have honey and which are brood nests. The capped cells that are darker and radiate from the center are brood, and the cells that are light (white) to golden-yellow are honey.

During the winter, many beekeepers will feed their bees a supplement of sugar water, or corn syrup and water. They can survive on this through the winter. I assume any viable individual bee can live on sugar water for up to three months, but a viable colony would need the complexities of nutrients that are offered from floral sources in order to raise their brood and continue the next generation.

There are three aspects that a beekeeper needs to effectively take care of for their bees: sharp senses, followed by a hive tool and a smoker. The worst thing any beekeeper can do is to be casual about it. Education is key to being successful.

Jason Gropple was president of the Montgomery County Beekeeping Association (MCBA) for the past five years and developed the MCBA Web site: www.mcbaonline.ning.com. He is a Tennessee apiary inspector and moderator for the Spanish language forum on www.beesource.com. He began beekeeping as a hobby five years ago.

Once all the preparations are made, place your bee order and be ready to install them in spring. Seasonal timing is significant if your bees are for-profit, but it is also essential for the bees' health and success. In early spring, U.S. bee breeders will have packaged bees for sale. These first bees of the season are ideal for new beekeepers.

Getting a late start in the bee season could mean that your bees will have a hard time surviving.

THE BeeKeePer BUZZ

"Spring is the best time to install the bees and to begin actual beekeeping," said beekeeper Charles Parton. "Use the winter months to begin building hives and to choose the location for the hives. For those who decide to purchase hives, do your homework and shop around for the best place to make a purchase."

Bees in their hive are similar to other animals in their home environment, even humans. There is a perfect time for everything; doing things out of this natural order can be a big disturbance and even deadly to the entire colony.

Chapter 3
Working the Hive

When it comes to working the hive, think of yourself as its CEO. It is your responsibility to troubleshoot problems, address worker needs, and create an environment that supports happy and productive workers.

It is important to have as much of your research, reading, and equipment prepared as possible before starting your work. Go to work dressed and ready for hive work wearing your bee suit, gloves, veil, and boots, and always have your tools (hive tool, smoker, and fuel) handy.

The Installation

The best time to install your bees is in early spring. The time when they are installed to the time there is substantial comb activity and hive life spans about two to three months. June is the time when there is a strong brood and a good amount of stored honey, nectar, pollen, and water.

To install the bees, remove the top portion of the hive. At this point, the frames and the brood box should be visible. To make room for the queen, push the frames apart and leave a gap in the middle.

Open the package of bees by carefully removing the staples in the lid with a hive tool. Be careful not to jar the package too much, or the bees will become agitated. Give them a few sprays of a sugar-water solution to distract them.

Inside the package is a metal tab; this tab connects to the queen's cage. The cage may be covered in workers, but this is natural. The workers have an ingrained need to cluster near and protect their queen. Again, give them a light spray of sugar water and gently tap the cage on the package. The bees will fall into the package.

Also within the package is a feeder can. This is what the bees used as a food supply during the trip. Take a hive tool and pry the can out of the package.

Gently replace the feeder can to hold the bees in place long enough to release the queen. Inside the queen's cage is a candy plug. The workers will be busy with the plug while the queen's pheromones are working. Remove the cork covering the candy cap with a pair of needle-nose pliers. Insert the queen's cage into the hive in between the frames; it should fit snugly, and the top should be flush with the frames.

The workers will continue to eat the candy plug and eventually release the queen. By this time, the queen should have been able to release enough pheromones to have her hive under control.

Remove the feeder can again. There may be a few workers hanging onto the can at this time; gently brush them into the hive. Take the package of bees by both hands and turn them upside down over the hive, where the queen box has been inserted. With a fast, downward shake, dump the bees into the hive. The bees should fall onto the frames in the hive — they should not fall onto the ground around the hive. Take special care not to hit the frames with the package because this will unnecessarily agitate the bees. Shake one or two times at the most. Do not worry about any dead bees; bees are their own undertakers and will dispose of their dead. There will be several bees left inside the package, but do not be concerned. Simply place the open end of the package against the opening of the hive. The bees will take their time getting into the hive.

If there is a feeder box in use, now is the time to put it to work. Feeder boxes slide onto the brood box. If not, simply place your top on the hive. It is a good idea to place a rock or brick on top of the hive to keep out raccoons, possums, skunks, and other small animals. It also gives extra weight in case of high winds and a storm. Do not lift the top or attempt to open the hive for seven to 10 days. This will only disturb the bees in their quest to develop a new comb.

Opening the Hive

After your initial visit, it is important to inspect the hive once a week. One of the biggest mistakes new beekeepers make is not inspecting the hive regularly. Do not open the hive every day or every other day because this disturbs the bees' natural order of things. Leave the bees to their own business. Working the hive does not mean opening the hive. Opening the hive disturbs the honey production, hive life, and may even kill a few bees each time. It pays to be vigilant. If during a weekly inspection any of the following conditions are noted, take action:

- **There is an odor**

  If there is a nasty smell in the apiary, there is a good possibility that your bees have contracted American foulbrood disease. If there is a faint smell of decaying fruit, particularly reminiscent of oranges, that could signal small-hive beetle infestation.

- **There is low foraging when there is high nectar flow**

  If your mature hive has foragers returning at a rate of less than one per second, there might be something wrong. If the colony is young, there will be fewer foragers, but a mature colony should have one or more bees returning per second. Low foraging rates can be a sign of tracheal mites or a stressful situation inside the hive.

- **There are dead or weak bees or larvae at the entrance to the hive**

  This is a sign of tracheal or varroa mites. Inspect the hive for more evidence of these pests.

- **There is a spill or topple**

  If someone or something has caused a physical disturbance in the hive, immediately open it and inspect for damage.

- **A new queen is in town**

  If a new queen is introduced into the hive, it is important to check on her within 24 hours. Then, after one or two weeks of her reign, recheck the hive. This is also a good time to recheck the candy plug. Sometimes the workers will be unable to remove it completely, and the queen will not be able to enter into her kingdom. *For more information about queening your hive, see Chapter 1.*

- **Swarm control techniques have been employed**

  Precautions such as removing queen cells, replacing the queen, and adding more brood boxes will slow down the tendency to swarm. Adding more brood boxes is also necessary when the hive has become overgrown. The bees naturally keep their honey and their brood separate, but as the hive grows, they will require more supers and brood boxes.

Things to Check For

When inspecting the hive, it is important to check the health of the bees, especially the queen. Take a look at the capped honey cells inside; this shows how active your bees are. Each frame should be filled from the middle outward The farther toward the outside the cells are, the more active and productive your bees are. Check the upcoming brood size by also checking the brood boxes. Move slowly and gently by softly nudging worker bees out of the way with a soft flower or piece of foliage — never shake or push them away roughly. Gently remove the brood frames and inspect for eggs or mites.

Inspecting the hive

Seasoned beekeepers call inspecting the hive "going through the bees." Careful and diligent management and routine inspections are the best practices when it comes to keeping disease and pests away. Know what to look for; learn the visual signs of trouble.

The best time to do this is during a warm and sunny day when most bees are out foraging. Bees forage during the morning hours when the sun first warms the air. The house bees left in the hive will be mostly youngsters without fully formed stingers. They are also busy during this time and not easily distracted, and they will likely stay on task once they are used to their hive being periodically inspected and opened.

Take an inner frame from the brood box and inspect it closely for the beginnings of comb and the small, translucent eggs that mean the life or death of your colony. Start at the middle of the frame and look outward. Keep the frame vertical to keep anything from falling out of the uncapped cells. Inspect the frame and comb by holding it directly over the box. If anything falls out, it will fall into the box. Be sure not to drop the queen.

If it appears that the queen's cage has caused a gap between the frames, the bees may have built burr comb to seal the opening. Scrape the burr comb from the sides by gently using your hive tool. Let the bees reclaim their property by placing the burr comb in the next available frame.

Identify eggs

Bee eggs are tiny — only about 2 millimeters long. It is important to be able to find and identify eggs because that is a key factor in determining the health and well-being of your queen. It is a skill you must develop well and become adept at, because you will use it time and time again.

THE BeeKeeper BUZZ

"Identifying eggs is important, and the first thing you need is sharp eyesight," said Cathie Skove, a New Jersey beekeeper. "The second is knowledge — know what you are looking for."

What makes them hard to see is not just the fact that they are tiny, but also their placement inside the cell. They are standing straight up on end. Looking down into the cells, you will see only the tiny tops of the egg. They are also translucent in their early stages and nearly invisible except for a small slice of iridescent light.

One way to spot eggs is to hold the comb at an angle and allow the sun to shine directly into the cells. The eggs are a milky, translucent color and will reflect in the sun. The use of a magnifying glass or high-powered reading glasses can help.

It is possible to have more than one egg in each cell. If that occurs, the problem could be a drone-laying queen, or it could mean that the queen is missing and now worker bees are laying eggs because they are confused about the roles that they are supposed to play. Neither are ideal situations. Drone-laying queens must be replaced immediately. Drone-laying workers need to be removed, and a new queen needs to be brought on board. Doing nothing and ignoring the situation will result in the annihilation of the colony.

New beekeepers run the risk of confusing the eggs of certain pests with the actual bee eggs. The young eggs of the wax moth and other pests can sometimes look like bees' eggs. Leaving a cluster of pests' eggs can be extremely detrimental to your hive.

The Dreaded Sting

Every beekeeper gets stung; it is part of the beekeeper's life. New beekeepers get stung more often than the pros, but that is only because of their initial nervousness when working the bees. Knowing how to effectively deal with stings is an important part of being a beekeeper.

The stinging apparatus itself comprises a venom sac, and the muscles that move it are attached to a shaft. The shaft has hollow, barbed lancets that carry the poison from the venom sac into the sting site. Once the stinger is inserted into the skin, its barbs become lodged in the skin and the stinger remains. Only the queen bee has the ability to sting repeatedly.

It is important to know how to remove a stinger. Because of the barb in the lancets, pulling out a stinger causes the venom sac to be squeezed, and more poison enters the skin. The recommended method of removing a stinger is to scrape it off with a fingernail or similar flat edge. Scraping instead of pulling lessens the amount of venom deposited into the sting site and thus lessens the effects of the poison.

For those who are allergic to bee stings and experience severe body reactions that could be life-threatening, apiculture may not be for you. There is no antidote that works fast enough for those individuals, and there is no way to 100 percent avoid getting a sting.

A big part of bee sting treatment is prevention. Bees will sting as a means to protect their hive or themselves. A novice beekeeper must learn how to approach the hive correctly to prevent unnecessary stings. If bees do not feel threatened, they will have less reason to sting. However, they are known to be particularly irritable in fall; treat them with respect to prevent unnecessary stings.

Bees are attracted to scents. After all, they look for flowers to do their life's work. Do not wear hairspray, perfume, or scented deodorant. Wash your bee suit and clothing with a detergent that has no scent. Do not use scented soaps, lotions, or oils before approaching your hives. It is also a good idea to dress in drab colors.

Do not bring food into the apiary. Under no circumstances should you bring soda or any drinks into the apiary — they are bee magnets.

After a sting, carefully remove the stinger and immediately wash the area with soap and water. One trick some beekeepers swear by is applying a thin layer of odorless antiperspirant to the sting site. There is an ingredient in antiperspirant called aluminum chlorohydrate that has adverse effects on the venom of bees. Other treatments include applying a cold press of ice or cold water, rubbing in calamine lotion, using a paste of baking soda and water, or an over-the-counter medication called acetaminophen or paracetamol.

A person who is not allergic will experience pain, red-ness, and considerable swelling — the swelling can actu-ally become alarming. But it stops there for most people. People who are allergic to bee stings will experience quite a different reaction. They get the initial hives, redness, swell-ing, and pain, but in seconds, the venom can go beyond the sting site to other parts of the body. It can be accom-panied by slurred speech, vomiting, dizziness, hoarseness, and difficulty breathing. Even a person who is not allergic to bee venom can experience extreme reactions if he or she is stung in the eyes and nose by ten or more bees. A doctor should be consulted in these cases.

Harvesting

Honey bees naturally make more honey than they need for themselves. In fact, if the beekeeper keeps adding more honey supers, the bees will continue to make honey, end-ing up with more honey than they could possibly use.

Harvesting is an essential beekeeping duty. It must be done or the hive will become crowded with honeycomb, and bees will swarm to find a new home. If honey is left in the comb, bees will stop or slow down on their honey production, but it is important to be able to tell when har-vesting should be done. If it is done too early or too late, problems can occur.

Harvesting honey too early causes spoilage. Young honey contains too much water and will ferment and spoil. You can sometimes find swollen jars of honey, which is a sign of fermentation. Those cannot be salvaged and must be thrown away. That is a waste of your time and money, as well as the bees' hard work. Make sure you know when to harvest your honey to prevent this unfortunate incident from happening.

Honey left in the comb too long will not spoil, but it does present other problems. It can turn a dark brown, which is usually off-putting to honey buyers. Most honey buyers prefer the golden-yellow color, and it is harder to get the honey out of the comb as well. Honey that has been in the comb a long time is thicker and will be resistant to extracting.

The honey is ready to be harvested when approximately 75 percent of the honey cells are capped in a frame. They cap their honey-filled cells with wax to signal that it is ripe and ready to be used. Do not harvest the honey before the frame is almost completely full, because the honey will spoil.

Honey that has been extracted from the comb is called extracted honey; honey left in the comb is comb honey, and a mixture of the two is called chunk honey. Chunk honey is a highly sought-after commodity; people enjoy having their honey in a lovely glass jar with a large chunk of comb inside. It gives the honey a special look and taste.

Make sure the capped cells have honey in them and not brood. The brood cells are convex because they provide room for the brood to develop from eggs to pupa and then larvae. When preparing to harvest the honey, remove the honey-filled frames from the hive. This is the first step in harvesting, and it is best to do this in the morning on a sunny, warm day when the majority of the hive is out foraging. Make sure to have all your equipment handy when beginning this process.

THE BEEKEEPER BUZZ

"There are just a bunch of tools I can't work without," said Ilse Ackermann, a beekeeper from California. "A smoker, a good hive tool, a bee brush, and I do wear a veil and gloves when I handle my bees, but I'm wimpy about stings. There are bee repellents, like Bee Gone™, which are great for emptying out a super when you want to retrieve honey. They have a revolting smell, but it works."

Bring an empty box to carry away the frames, and do not lay them on the ground. Ants and other insects love honeycomb, and it will not take long for the honeycomb to become full of hungry bugs. Bring a cloth to cover the frames and to deter bees from working on them while they are being freed from the hive.

Remove the frames one at a time, slowly. More than three-fourths of the cells should have a wax cap. Be careful and look for brood; try to avoid removing brood at all costs, as they are the future of your colony. The cells should be flat and capped with a white wax top. To determine a brood, use your hive tool and scrape one or two cappings off. Look for gorgeous, golden-yellow honey inside.

THE BeeKeeper BUZZ

"It is not always easy to tell which of the capped cells have honey and which have brood," said Ilse Ackermann, a veteran California beekeeper. "This has to do with color for me. The honey looks like, well, honey, and the brood is darker. Brood is usually in the middle/bottom of frame, and honey scattered around the outer edges."

It is also important to check out each of the bees on the frames. Make sure the queen is not on one of the frames. If the queen is not visible, and if there are any remaining bees on the frame, gently brush them back into the hive with a bee brush or a soft flower. The key word is *gently*. Never shake, push, or roughly remove the bees from their frames.

Harvesting honey with an extractor is one way to remove the honey from the cells. Cut the caps from the cells with your uncapping tool by carefully sliding it along the top of the frame's capped cells, then put the frames into the extractor. Extractors are hand-operated or electric. They spin the frames until a majority of the honey is removed. The honey is run through a filtration system and stored in a tank. Hand-cranked extractors require hard work, but are considerably less expensive than the electric extractor.

If the cost of the extractor is an issue, there are several ways to get honey out of the comb without using a centrifuge extractor. Remove the caps and lean a warm comb frame at an angle in a clean tub. Allow the honey to drain slowly into the tub for several hours. When all the honey has been drained out, replace the comb frames into the hive. The bees repair the comb and tidy up the remaining honey before beginning to fill them again.

If the bees do not reuse the comb, place the honey-filled frames into a big tub. Scrape the comb from the cells all the way down to the foundation with a steel or plastic spatula. Dip the spatula in a pan of boiling water between scrapings to make it easier to cut through the hardened wax. It is possible to use an electric uncapping knife. Be careful, as they are extremely hot.

Honey left in the comb is more valuable because it has a richer taste. To package comb honey, use a sharp knife or the un-capping knife to cut hunks of the comb and insert immediately into the jars. Make sure to tightly cap the jars when finished, and wipe the outside with a warm, soapy cloth to remove any honey residue that will attract insects, dust, and dirt particles.

The Bee Year

Knowing how your bees live and work is one thing, but it is just as important, if not more so, to know *when* things happen. A bee year begins in the winter. The bees will have stored a stock supply of honey to live off all winter. They have been huddled in the center of their hive together to conserve body heat while doing their daily chores.

If the winters are cold, your bees have had a rough few months. They must raise brood; even small brood nests are important. In order to do this in the winter, they must keep the hive warm. Expending body energy means shortening their life spa, thus some beekeepers will insulate the hives. This is a fairly easy chore that can save the colony from dying. Simply wrap the hive in a soft, warm cloth and cover the entire hive with a tarp. It is also a good idea to leave a ramp at the hive entrance. Angle a board from the hive entrance directly to the ground to help the bees get in and out of the hive while it is wrapped.

Bees will not emerge until temperatures reach at least 50°. Instead, they cluster deep in the hive, conserving body heat and raising small batches of brood. They break between batches and rest to replenish their strength. Once the weather allows for fresh pollen to make its way into the hive, the colony will begin reproducing in earnest. It is also possible to put out pollen patties to aid in the process. The bees must go out to forage even in the cold weather, but if the weather is cold for a prolonged time, a colony could starve to death. Use pollen patties close to the hive entrance. These are sugar boards, called "bee candy" or "winter candy."

Many beekeepers will continue to feed their bees far into the spring when natural food sources are available. This is done to increase brood rearing. When extra food is given for this purpose, extra pollen should also be supplied. It is important not to supply these extras too early in the spring. If the bees are encouraged to build larger brood nests and it is still cold, they will end up with a large, dead brood. They may not be able to keep the hive warm enough to keep the brood alive, and once the brood dies, the over-worked workers will be susceptible to illnesses and pests. It is best to wait until the first bloom of spring.

During winter, there are many things to be done for the bees and the hives. While they are clustered close together deep in the hive, they slowly move over the honey-filled combs and eat the food inside. It is important not to open the hives at this time of year. It is hard work for the bees to maintain the proper temperature inside the hives. Keep an eye on the outside of the hives; make sure there is no weather damage or leaks into the hive. Check that all rodent blocks are still in place. If a mouse or other rodent enters the hive in winter, it can mean death for the whole colony. Winter is also the perfect time for repairing broken hives or building new ones — there is no better way to cut costs and increase profit than making your own hives.

It is also a good idea to use the winter months to clean tools and repair damaged ones; review records and jour-nals; market your products; or find new clients. This is also a good time to compare notes with other beekeepers from around the area.

In February, some early bloomers begin to wake, and the bees sense life stirring in the world around them. The tem-peratures will begin to rise slightly, and the queen will start to lay small clusters of eggs in the cells at the center of their bee huddle. Once the brood-raising begins and the temper-ature reaches at least 46°, the bees will take short cleans-ing flights and set out on short journeys to find water.

In most areas of the country, by the time March comes along, the bees are more active. It is warm enough during late February and early March to remove insulation around the hive, and the bees will be come and go more frequently. On the first warm day in the upper 50s, the hive can be opened for its first inspection of the year. Check for signs of illnesses or pests; make sure there is enough fresh water and food; and check the status of the brood. Do not forget to locate the queen on this first inspection. If there is no brood, there will be no queen, so it will be important to requeen as soon as possible. By the first real bloom of spring, your hive should have had at least one full brood emerge and be well on its way to more.

THE BeeKeeper BUZZ

"I recommend locating a beekeeping association in your area and attend the spring short course, or at least a few meetings to learn some necessities," said beekeeper Lynda Cook Rizzardi. "Then, plan to begin with a hive in the spring — follow through with monthly maintenance, learning activities, and hopefully reap a harvest of delicious sweetness from your labor of love."

By April and May, the hive should be bustling with changes. The old bees that lived through the winter are dying off, and the young bees are replacing them. More brood are being raised, and the bees continue to forage for food to feed their young. The act of raising brood requires more food, so the bees are constantly foraging and bringing in food and water. This is still a dangerous time of year for the bees because weather temperatures can fluctuate and become deadly for them.

During May and June, the colony is functioning at full capacity. More than 80 percent of the hive is full of brood and honey supers. Swarming often happens during this time of year because the hives get full. Check the hive often to see what the bees are planning.

Beekeepers love the summer — this is when the honey flows freely for home use or to sell. New beekeepers are always amazed at the beauty of fresh, ripe honey. But rain can affect your honey flow in the summer, and so can a pollen drought. Pay attention to weather conditions, and be prepared to offer your colony assistance. By summer, the bees are expanding at a fast pace. Check their spaces regularly, add extra supers when needed, and make sure the brood nest is large enough.

By the end of July, the dangers of swarming have passed, and the drones will be driven off by the worker bees. Most of the foraging is done from honeydew, so foraging flights are done early in the morning and late evenings. Robbing occurs at this time of year when wild swarms find themselves low on food and pollen. Make sure the bees have enough natural food; if not, provide a substitute.

In fall, the foraging begins to slow down. There might be one fall honey flow, but usually the queen stops laying, and the hive begins to settle in for the winter. The bees that will carry the hive through winter are being born. The larger this hatching of brood, the better chance the colony has of surviving the winter. The more bees to winter means the hive will stay warmer and longer through the winter; once spring arrives, there will be more bees to emerge alive and begin foraging.

In September, the hive gets smaller because the bees that die at this time of year are not replaced. Take any empty combs out of the hive and store them for the winter. Take one last look at your bees for the winter before temperatures begin to fall. During October and November, take precautions against small rodents and pests.

In December, the bees will be clustered into a tight ball in the center of their hive. They feed on the food and honey that they have gathered all summer. The bees tend to their small broods and conserve heat and energy. This is a good month to weatherproof the hives. Make sure all leaks are sealed and cracks are filled in; paint them if need be. *For a complete beekeeping calendar, see Appendix A.*

Moving a Hive

Moving a hive is often necessary. Some beekeepers will move a hive as the seasons change, taking the hive a few miles to a more productive nectar flow. Others will transport bees to other states for seasonal purposes or for shipping to a buyer.

Begin to move the hive before dawn, when all of your bees are safely inside. Cover the entrance of the hive with a length of wire screen. The screen shuts off the entrance to the hive but leaves plenty of ventilation. Place the screen over the entrance and then, using your hand or a bee-keeper's tool, gently push the screen into the entrance hole until it covers the entire opening.

When transporting bees by vehicle, make sure the beehive is secured inside. Use a bungee cord or rope to tie down the hive and keep it from sliding around or toppling over.

Problems that can Occur With Beekeeping

Beekeeping is not without its problems. Some issues are more devastating to the colony and hive than others. As a beekeeper, it is your duty to be able to recognize these problems when they happen and, if possible, stop them. Some of the potential problems include disease and illnesses, pest and mite problems, or missing queens or runaway bees. Thankfully, bees survive most of these issues, and some can be prevented with expert planning.

Sickness

Bees are hardy, industrious, and clean. They work to keep their hive and colony free of disease. They immediately remove their dead and the dead of intruders, if possible. If not, they cover the remains with propolis.

There are certain maladies that affect bees and can cause illness or death to the colony, including the brood. Many illnesses that affect bees are called stress diseases, such as not enough food or water; other maladies are natural bacteria and viruses common to honey bees. Some of the diseases can be stopped if caught in time, but others can be a death sentence — no matter when they are discovered.

Nosema

This quiet killer has often been compared to high blood pressure in humans. The symptoms are so slight that the disease often goes undetected until the entire colony has been affected. The disease is caused by the protozoan *Nosema apis*. It spreads throughout the colony by way of spores and affects the host's digestive system. If infected bees are stuck inside the hive because of prolonged inclement weather and cannot take a cleansing flight, they defecate inside the hive, leaving disease-spreading spores. Nosema causes the bee to have difficulty digesting food, and it competes for the bees' nutrients. In workers, the disease impedes the ability to produce brood food, causes premature aging, and shortens the worker's lifespan by at least 10 percent.

When the queen is affected, the whole colony becomes aware. An affected queen will be superseded in two to three weeks tops. She will slowly begin losing her ability to digest food and properly use the nutrients. Her egg-laying capabilities will diminish, and the colony will start to take action.

This illness is spread from one colony to another by drifting bees, often in early spring. It is also spread by borrowing equipment from other beekeepers. Keep the tool borrowing to a minimum, or partake in none at all. If this disease is not addressed immediately, it can destroy an entire colony. Keep the spread of spores down by following these tips:

- Use fumagillin in the fall to inhibit spore germination.

- Make sure your packager and breeder treat for the disease and take precautions against it.

- Keep bee stressors to a minimum.

- Refrain from exchanging frames or other equipment with neighboring colonies.

Chalkbrood

Have you ever seen powdery mildew on the leaves of a plant in the garden? This is similar to chalkbrood for bees, except it grows on the brood. When a larva comes in contact with the chalkbrood spores, it is starved to death. The spores germinate, eventually work their way into the insides of the larva, and consume all of the nutrients, gradually killing it and covering the entire cell. The larvae become tiny mummies visible on the running board of the hive or on the ground surrounding the hive. Chalkbrood prospers with the fluctuation of temperatures in the spring and will most likely be found at the edge of the brood nest, where temperature fluctuations are most noticeable.

Currently, there is no chemical treatment for this malady. There are many regular management techniques that can be employed to slow, stop, and prevent the disease from making an impact on your colony. If your breed of bees is hygienic, they will do much of the work themselves, cleaning the infected cells and depositing the mummified remains out of the hive. Your job then is to remove and destroy affected frames and replace them with new ones.

CASE STUDY: HANDLING PROBLEMS FOR SUCCESSFUL BEEKEEPING

Cathie Skove

There are several problems that can occur that make beekeeping difficult: bad weather, bee and brood diseases, and pests are some of the worst. The weather presents a problem if it is too dry, wet, or cold because the nectar production can be impaired.

When I began keeping bees, there were no mites and only one medication to deal with. Now, you practically have to be a doctor, scientist, and forest ranger to be successful.

There are no absolutes when it comes to keeping disease and pests away. Your best defense is knowledge. It is important to be able to identify your problem before it can be treated. Some diseases are curable if found in time, but they can still be troublesome. If not found in time, they can kill a hive and spread to an entire apiary. Pests that cause problems include bears, raccoons, possums, birds, and internal and external mites.

Identifying eggs is an important part of beekeeping. The tiny eggs look like minute grains of rice in the bottom center of a wax cell. In about three days, they go from standing to lying down in the bottom of the cell. Two books that can help with egg identification are *The Hive and the Honey Bee*, and *ABC/XYZ of Beekeeping*.

The best time of year to begin beekeeping is after the first frost of the preceding season. Begin by reading and or taking classes to learn what you are doing before your bees arrive.

The question of how much honey to take and how much to leave for bees to survive on depends on your state. A cell capped with wax has honey; it is translucent and shows the honey is light or dark. A brood cell is darker, tan or brownish, slightly fibrous, and slightly domed for worker (female) brood; it is sharply domed for drone (male) brood.

Bees can survive on the sugar water forever, if necessary. Sugar water made with 1-to-1 or 2-to-1 ratio is closer to nectar than honey and actually preferred by bees. Although bees can survive on sugar water, brood cannot. It requires protein that comes from pollen collected in the spring, summer, and fall foraging months. The length of time that a colony can last without a queen depends on the time of the year; bees live 5 to 6 weeks in summer, and 6 to 8 months over winter.

As for protective gear — a bee suit, jacket, veil, and gloves — the choice is up to the beekeeper. When I just started out, I used the full suit; now, I always use a veil and only add gloves and suits if necessary.

Cathie Skove has been a beekeeper for 30 years and held offices in two local chapters in New Jersey state bee organizations.

European foulbrood

Nurse bees accidentally spread this disease to the colony's larvae. European foulbrood is a bacterium known as *Melissococcus pluton.* It attacks the young larvae and begins to steal the nutrients from the food. The larvae die, melting into a rubbery pile at the bottom of the cell. If there is a brood frame with holes throughout it, that is a sign that European foulbrood is the culprit. When the house bees clean the infected cells, they acquire the spores and unknowingly transfer them to waiting larvae.

European foulbrood is commonly found in hives that are under stress. The less stress on a hive, the lower the chances are of contracting this disease; therefore, keep plenty of food and water available. Remove old frames and replace them with new ones if this disease is a recurring problem. This disease can be treated with an antibiotic.

American foulbrood

American foulbrood is a deadlier cousin of the European foulbrood. The bacteria *Paenibacillus* is the cause of this deadly malady. This is the most destructive and costly of all the diseases that affect bees, and it takes the most drastic measures to rid a colony of it.

This disease will affect the colony when its spores are brought into the colony. This can be done in any number of ways. If your bees rob a colony that is contaminated by American foulbrood, they can bring the spores back. It can also be spread by the use of contaminated equipment.

Like the other major bee diseases, the spores of American foulbrood are swallowed and then go to work in the gut. Once the cell is capped over, the infected larvae will die, and the bacterium feeds off the dead larvae. Once fully consumed, the larvae become a hardened mass of the bacterium spores that diligently adhere to the cell walls. It is so tough to get rid of that worker bees often cannot remove it.

This is a serious disease and, in most states, the Department of Agriculture has regulations on the treatments and controls. To date, the only legal antibiotic available is Ter-ramycin, registered by Pfizer, Inc., which is usually available at bee supply houses. Many beekeepers choose to destroy the colony and equipment instead of using the chemical. This is a drastic step, but often the most effective.

Drifting

Drifting is when bees leave their colony and enter a neighboring colony. This happens in an apiary where there is more than one colony. It is not a major problem unless more bees leave than come back, or if diseases are spread. If all the drifting bees do not return home, this can reduce the strength of the donor colony quite a bit.

Robbing

Robbing occurs when bees steal honey from a hive other than their own. The stronger hives rob the weaker or queenless hives — queenless hives are more likely to be robbed than those that are queenright.

All species are prone to this behavior, but the Italian species are more vulnerable than others. This usually happens when the flow of nectar in the area is low. Sometimes this is done so deftly that it goes unnoticed. Other times, especially in an apiary, rival bees will fight over the robbing of honey. This can lead to all-out warfare and a considerable loss of bees.

Feeding the colony man-made food is not always a cure, and it can actually exacerbate the problem. The most effec-

tive action against robbing is good, old-fashioned prevention. Simple tasks like minimizing the entrance to the hive
during a drought can be the best thing to stop robbing
bees, in addition to closing the entrance at night. Robbing
bees will show up in the early morning hours when it is
still cool.

THe BeeKeeper BUZZ

"I also had robbing early on, probably because there is a wild hive that must be close
to my hives," said California beekeeper Ilse Ackermann. "The bees become really agitated when they are being robbed, and they can really come at you. What I did to stop
that was immediately throw a damp sheet over the hives; the bees can still get in, but
it stops the robbers right away. Now when I open a hive, I spray a couple of squirts
of liquid smoke into the air, and that disguises the smell of honey in the hive. Vicks®
VaporRub can be used above the entrance to disguise the smell as well. I had a swarm
last spring that I managed to catch and rehive; that was an adventure."

Stuffing the opening with grass can close the opening for
a few days, but the bees will remove it. It is hoped that the
robbers will tire of trying to get in by then. There are cloths
that can be used to wrap the hives in for up to 72 hours if
they have proper ventilation — robbers will tire of trying to
gain entrance by then.

Though these solutions will slow down and stop robbing
bees, they have little effect on your colony. It might slow
down their daily activities, but more damage can come
from the problems than the solutions.

Orientation flights are often mistaken for robbing bees by
new beekeepers. New bees out for a first fly will be fuzzy:

They will float gently and land easily; they will crawl slowly on the hive and enter peacefully. Robbing bees are the opposite: They are harried; they dart the hive and land on the hive front; they scramble, fight, and wrestle to the entrance.

It is important to recognize the warning signs of this phenomenon. If nothing seems to be able to stop the robbing, it might be necessary to combine two hives or move the hive to another location.

Pests

Honey bees are not native to the United States, so they have no natural enemies. There are many varmints and insects, however, that can cause them considerable problems. There are no absolutes when it comes to keeping disease and pests away. Your best defense is knowledge. It is important to be able to identify your problem before it can be treated. Some diseases are curable if found in time, but they can still be troublesome. If not found in time, they can kill a hive and spread to an entire apiary. Pests that cause problems include bears, raccoons, possums, birds, and internal and external mites, according to bee expert Cathie Scove.

Bears

Bears often pose a problem for honey bee colonies. A bear will repeatedly return to a hive to eat all the honey and brood. Unfortunately, bee stings have no affect on the bear. The best defense against a bear is to install an electric fence around the hive, or a sturdy fence or cage that the bear cannot destroy. Another option is to relocate the hive — because once a determined bear has discovered an apiary, it will continue to be a problem.

Small rodents

Mice can cause a serious problem in a hive. They move in during colder months when the colony is preparing to cluster for the winter. They chew combs and frames to make their nests. The bees take little notice of them until spring, but the urine of mice, shrews, or moles will make the bees reluctant to clean their nest. To control small rodent infestations, use wire mesh or wooden or metal pieces to reduce the entrance to bee size.

Farm animals

Farm animals are not a direct threat to a bee colony, but pose a different kind of hazard. They will often attempt to scratch against the hive or otherwise knock it over, causing considerable damage. Bees are also a source of possible problems for livestock, especially horses. Bees can buzz around them and make them nervous and hard to handle. The best way to handle bees and livestock is to locate the apiary behind a fence or make the bees inaccessible to the animals.

Small mammals

Skunks, raccoons, and possums can find an apiary and instantly have a honey-bee buffet. Their plan of attack includes scratching and clawing at the hive so that guard bees come out to investigate. When they emerge, they are instantly pawed to the ground and eaten, Not only is the population of bees being diminished, but each time the hive is disturbed, they become more agitated. To control the risk of trouble from these types of pests, consider putting the hive up on a pedestal. If the animals are standing on hind legs to scratch at the hive, it exposes their tender underbelly and face so that it receives the stings. This is a big deterrent. A sturdy fence and elevation of the hives will most often do the trick.

Toads and frogs

These pests are big insect eaters. They are a more serious pest to the bee in areas near the Caribbean Islands.

Ants

Ants are not a threat to bees, but they pose more of a problem to a beekeeper during hive inspection. Ants will nest inside the hive, and if bees can get near them, they will get rid of them by stinging and killing them. One reason you should try to avoid letting ants near your colony is because the ants can eat the honey, and the ants could also hurt the bees. To prevent either of these things from happening, you can try moving colonies, but if ants are a serious problem, the best deterrent is to place the hive on a stand with the legs in buckets of vegetable oil.

Birds

Lots of birds dine on bees, but it is not possible for a whole colony of bees to be wiped out by birds. Colonies are fully equipped to survive the occasional loss to a bird. The real threat from birds comes if the bird happens to eat a queen on a mating flight, or if a woodpecker comes calling. Woodpeckers have been known to target a hive and eat bees as they come and go. The green woodpecker might be the biggest pest of all the birds because once it discovers the hive, it will peck fist-sized holes in the hive in less than an hour's time. It will eat wax, honey, and bees. One solution is to wrap the hive in chicken wire several times. This way, the bees can fly in and out, but the birds cannot. Because most bees do not sting unless provoked, the birds are usually not threatened by the bees in the hive.

Lepidoptera (moths)

These insects are known for their four wings that are covered completely in scales. The scales give the wings distinguishing patterns and colors. Butterflies are a well-known member of this insect family. Though they are not harmful to bees, their brothers and sisters in this insect family — the death's-head hawkmoths (*Acherontia atropos*) — are a notorious enemy to bees. They are similar to the wax moth and can lay eggs in a hive that will destroy the entire hive and colony if left unchecked.

Moths can be a problem for a colony. They are after the pollen and honey but can destroy an entire hive in the process. Indian meal moths, Mediterranean flour moths, and wax moths will burrow into the hive and chew up the wax comb to get to the pollen and honey. Most often, the workers will remove the pupa and caterpillar silk when performing the house maintenance, but with a heavy infestation, the hive may get so weak from the burrowing moths that it collapses. A strong hive needs no outside help to eliminate these pests. They will attack and kill them, and remove the remains.

Spiders

Spiders are tiny predators out to kill any and all prey. Some spiders actively seek out their prey, attack, and devour it; others lie in wait for an unsuspecting insect to amble along to its death. These spiders can camouflage themselves against flowers and plants; others build snares like webs and trap doors. The spiders that threaten the honey bee are those that build webs. The black widow spider will go so far as to spin its web inside the hive. They build it between the top or bottom boards, or small cracks and crevices in the outer walls. Rev. Lorenzo Lorraine Langstroth, designer of the modern movable frame beehives, believed that spiders could be helpful to honey bee combs. He thought it was possible that spiders would aid the bees in patrolling the hive and protecting it against the damages of wax moths by killing them.

But exceptions to this theory are the orb weaver spider and the crab spider, both of which will attack and eat honey bees at every chance. The orb weaver captures the bees in their webs and devours them; crab spiders hide in or near flowers for worker bees out foraging.

Author's Apiary

Mites and foulbrood and bears...oh my!

There is probably more information available about the pests and diseases of honey bees than about the honey bee. The wonderment and joy of the age-old tradition of beekeeping as a hobby is often overshadowed by the fear of all the maladies associated with the husbandry of bees.

I remember very clearly my excitement of learning all there was to know about beekeeping so I could start my own apiary. However, after completing yet another class on bee diseases at the annual Bee College, excitement quickly turned to disappointment and concern about what I was getting myself into. Thank goodness a fellow "classmate" who would end up being my good friend and mentor must have understood what was happening. He quickly assured me that in his 12 years of beekeeping, he had to deal with only a fraction of the information that was being taught.

To know and understand all the possibilities that can, and sometimes do, arise is a smart way to go into beekeeping. Letting it spoil the fun is not. Enjoy!

Wasps

Wasps are angry little bullies. Yellow jackets and hornets will attack single foraging bees and groups of bees as well. They may also capture dying bees at the hive's entrance, and during colder temperatures, they will enter the hive and steal a meal of honey. Hornets are known to enter apiaries and make a meal of honey and worker bees in the colder months, and wasps are a brutal adversary for honey bees. This is a war that has waged for centuries, and bees can hold their own, but with a little help from their bee-keeper, they can win the battle, if not the war.

Many experienced beekeepers know that wasps seem to vary in numbers from year to year. But new beekeepers have not developed this innate sense of when wasps will be at their worst, so it is best to be cautious.

Flies

There are several species of flies that eat bees. Some are even named for their favorite meal, such as the southern bee killer and the Texas bee killer. The only solution known to work is to move the colony.

The braula is a fly that lives off bees. They ride around on the bee's back and, when hungry, cause the bee to feed them regurgitated honey. They do not harm the bees, but they can have an effect on honey supply because their larvae tunnel under honey cell cappings and make honey unfit for sale or use. On the other hand, robber flies are carnivorous. They eat not only bees, but a variety of insects, such as house flies, wasps, dragonflies, and grasshoppers.

Lice

Braula coeca, or bee lice, can pose a problem for your hives and colony. They are insects, but not true lice. These little insects are present all over the world. They are round and brick red. Their mouths suck, but are not capable of piercing. Their eyes are rudimentary, which are perfect for seeing inside the dark hives. They clasp the hairs on the bee's body and spend their entire lives there. Female bee lice lay their eggs on the underside of the honey cell cappings, and the larvae hatch facing down into the honey cell. When they hatch, they begin tunneling and eating throughout the honeycombs. They stay in these tunnels until they become adult bee lice. They can cause considerable harm to the honey and the queen, especially if there are large numbers of them. They prefer the queen because the workers bring her the best food on a regular basis. If your queen is covered in these tiny little hitchhikers, get rid of them by exposing them to tobacco smoke.

Mites

The biggest problem a bee will have from a pest are mites. There are three types of mites: parasitidae, thrombididae, and sarcoptidae. These tiny insect cousins can be a serious problem, but there are many types that are harmless. Mites of every type can invade a honey beehive, whether it is healthy, weak, or diseased. Many are detrimental simply because they destroy the pollen supplies and honey. They are not pathogenic to the bees. It is easier for the mites to get a strong foothold in a weak, diseased hive than a healthy one, as weak bees do not have the numbers to fight a strong infestation of mites.

Humid conditions are favorable to mites and produce the perfect environment for them to grow and gain strength inside a hive. Try to keep the hives and any stored wax, pollen, or honey in a cool and dry environment; this will keep the infestations to a minimum.

The tracheal mite, *Acarapis woodi*, causes the disease acarine, also known as the Isle of Wight disease because that is where it was first discovered. This mite kills the bee by entering a young bee's trachea and breeding there. It eventually causes a blockage, which considerably shortens a bee's life. This affects the whole colony because it is unable to repopulate by spring, and the dwindling colony cannot survive the winter. Grease patties and menthol fumigation are forms of control but are not always effective.

Varroa mites are a bigger problem. They live on developing and adult bees and will deform and eventually kill them. The adult and its young feed on the blood of honey bees. The adult varroa mites survive the winter attached to the body of its host honey bee. They will also sometimes spend their winter inside the brood nest of the hive. But what they do most successfully in the brood is reproduce. Pregnant varroa mites enter brood cells just moments before they are to be sealed. Once the cell is sealed, the mite feeds on the developing bee pupa and begins to lay its own eggs. The first egg of this type of mite is a female and the second is male. After that, each egg is a female. If the mites are tucked away in the cell of worker bee, they go through several life stages. The male mates with his sisters, then the oldest pregnant female eventually emerges from the cell tucked safely between the abdominal plates of the young bee. The remaining females and the lone male will die in the cell. If they were inside of a drone cell, which they prefer, then more than one pregnant female can emerge. In these cases, a colony can find itself with a drone brood and a bad case of varroa mites.

Although dead and deformed bees are a horrible consequence, there are other more insidious problems. A mite that feeds upon a bee infected with a virus can give that virus to another bee. The virus seems to get worse while it is carried in the mite.

There are forms of control, but this issue can spin into something uncontrollable and can demolish an entire colony. If a wild swarm gets an infestation of varroa, it will die within two years. A colony must be treated in order to be rid of this deadly infestation.

If you have determined that you do have a problem, there are several approved and effective chemicals (miticides) for varroa mites. You can try using Apistan (fluvalinate), CheckMite+ (foric acid), or Apiguard (thymol). Because the bees can develop a resistance to these medications, it is suggested that you alternate treatment each season. A few words of warning: Use protective gloves when handling any kind of chemical, and never treat your bees with any kind of medication when you have honey supers on the hive, as it will contaminate the honey for human consumption. The following descriptions will help you choose which chemical to use for protecting your hive:

- **Apistan** is packaged as strips that are placed between frames in the brood box. The bees come into contact with the medicated strips, brush up against each other, and transfer the fluvalinate through the hive.

- **CheckMite+** is also packaged as strips and placed between frames. It is the recommended treatment if your bees have become resistant to the Apistan. CheckMite+ can also used to treat a small hive beetle infestation.

- **Apiguard** is a slow-release gel mix. The gel comes in ready-to-use aluminum trays, which are placed on top of the brood box. The worker bees climb on the tray and begin to remove the gel as part of their hive cleaning. The gel sticks to their hairs and is transferred throughout the hive. Apiguard is also effective against tracheal mites and chalkbrood.

Other problems

Hive beetles

The scientific name for the small hive beetle is *Aethina tumida*. These beetles were originally from Africa. Young hive beetles are a yellowish brown and, as they become adults, turn to a dark brown or black. They appear to be segmented into three sections, with the middle wing section overlapping the head and tail area. They are very hard to pick up by hand because of their size, quickness, and small hairs over their bodies. They like to find weak or dead combs and scavenge the remaining honey and wax. They also survive in storage rooms that have stored honey. Keeping tools and equipment lying around that have honey and wax still on them is a surefire way to attract small hive beetles. It is important to keep the apiary clean, especially for this reason.

The eggs of the small hive beetles are similar to the eggs of the bees; they are only about 1.4 millimeters in length. Adult small hive beetles will lay their eggs in uneven clusters all throughout the hive, in any cracks and crevices in the wood, or in any stacks of equipment. The eggs will hatch in a week, typically. If the temperature is too low, the eggs will not hatch, and they also require a certain amount of humidity to hatch. Once the beetles have hatched, they begin to feed on the honey, bee eggs, pollen, and brood cells of the hive. They will eventually come out of the hive and burrow into the ground to pupate. Beetle larvae are also maggot-like in appearance. They do not eat the wax like the wax moth, but they will destroy an entire hive's honey supply as they eat through the combs. They ruin pollen supplies and the newly converted nectar.

If you have a strong hive, the bees can handle the beetles. They chase them out or corral them in corners and put guard bees on duty to keep them confined. Give your bees a little help and purchase a hive beetle trap.

Missing queen

There are several reasons a queen might go missing. But no matter the reason, it is important to be able to recognize the situation as soon as possible. If not, your entire colony is in jeopardy. Your colony could reject the queen. This sometimes happens when a new queen is introduced. They will reject her as an intruder and evict her from the hive. A queen could have a weak pheromone scent. If this is the case, she is considered weak by the colony and will be killed. If a queen is missing, it is important to replace her as soon as possible. The most problematic issue for new beekeepers is usually thinking they are without a queen, introducing a new queen, then finding that the hive has killed the new queen. Being able to recognize your queen is never more important than in this instance. If a beekeeper has trouble identifying the queen, it may be a good idea to mark her with a small dot of paint.

New beekeepers will sometimes hive a new package of bees and then, a few days later, be unable to find the queen. Remember not to panic. The queen will naturally run from light when the hive is opened. The best course of action is to search for her carefully and, if she does not appear in a few days, look for the eggs. They are a bit easier to identify. If there is no sight of the queen or any eggs, wait ten days and re-inspect the hive. At this time, the eggs will be larger, and some may be in pupa stage and be easier to find. If there is no sight of a queen, eggs, or brood at any stage, it is time to order a new queen. This time, place a white dot on her back before hiving her.

Bee Gardens

Planting a bee garden is a great addition to an apiary. A bee garden is used to attract bees, but oddly enough, not all flowers attract bees. Some flowers and flowering plants are better at attracting bees than others; therefore, it is a good idea to do some research before starting a bee garden. It is not possible to stop other insects from coming to visit, but it is possible to tailor your garden to bees specifically.

For example, hummingbirds and butterflies should be welcomed into your garden.

The next step is to choose a location for the garden. It might be good to place it as close to the hives as possible, or in an area that encourages flight away from neighbors. Designate as much space as possible for your bee garden — the bigger the better. It is best to have ten or more bee-attractive plants in order to encourage regular visits. Choose plants that bees might not put high on their list of favorites; if the plants are there in abundance, the bees will visit.

Another benefit to the bee garden is that it does not require a great deal of maintenance. Once the initial planning is done, there is not much work left other than occasionally watering and fertilizing, if necessary. That means no weeding and cultivating; the messier the garden, the better. Well-manicured and highly maintained bee gardens receive much less bee traffic than those allowed to progress naturally. Leaving some overgrowth gives the bees protection from their enemies, from the sun, and from pesticides. Predators and parasites have a much harder time preying on the working bees when they are given the chance to hide.

No weed killer or pesticides are needed, either, because they can ruin even the most attractive bee gardens. Even if local bees love the types of flowers and flowering plants you have planted, a dose or two of pesticide or weed killers can drive them away. This aspect of beekeeping is extremely important if you plan to sell your honey or if you plan to be recognized and designated as an organic or natural bee-keeper and provider of natural honey.

Do not get upset at the sight of other bugs. Ladybugs, ants, and praying mantises are a great help to your bee garden. They stave off pests like caterpillars that will eat the plants and other enemies to your bees. They also minimize the need for pesticides.

Plant your flowers and plants close together in squares of approximately 3 feet by 3 feet or larger. Leave small spaces between species of plants, and plant your next block of flowers. Usually, just 6 to 8 inches between species is sufficient. These spaces are almost as important as the flowers themselves. Try to use small pathways between the flowers in order to make daily checks of your garden.

It also helps to label each patch of flowers with its common and scientific names. Later, check your notes and compare which plants are best for your bees and your geographic location, and find other plants for the following season that are closely related. If there are unidentified plants, take a cutting to your local garden suppler and ask the experts.

When deciding which plants to use, there are a few points to consider. Choose plants that bloom at different times of year: spring, summer, fall, and winter. This keeps your bees with a steady supply of food. It might be difficult to find winter flowering plants, but it possible to provide food for your bees in other ways, such as sugar-water sprays and food additions available from bee suppliers.

Take a walk around your community and notice which plants are attracting bees. If they are already growing right in your community, they are accustomed to the area and the growing season. They evolved there and can make good use of the soil and climate. Local plants require less watering and care than something new. Also, buying plants from a grower or plant supplier can pose a small problem. Most plants are grown simply for their aesthetics and not necessarily for their benefits for pollinators like bees. Local, wild plants provide a more rich nutritional value for the bees.

Be sure to have a water source for your garden. If your bee garden is a longer distance from your apiary, set up a dripping faucet, birdbath, or other source of clean, fresh water for your busy, pollinating bees.

One thing to keep in mind is to only plant single varieties of plants. Some flowers are termed as "doubles," which means that they have been altered genetically to develop extra petals instead of anthers and will therefore produce little pollen. Flowers that most people would think attract many bees, like roses and marigolds, will not attract any bees if they are doubles.

These types of flowering plants and trees are attractive to most bees:

Annuals

Annuals are plants that complete an entire life cycle in one year. There are certain annuals that are more attractive to bees than others. These include sunflowers — which are often food for specializing bees — poppies, zinnias, asters, calliopsis, marigolds, and clover.

Perennials

Perennials are plants that live for more than two years. These types of plants will appear to die but are really hibernating until the time comes to sprout and bloom again. There are many perennial plants that bees love. Just like with annuals, if the plant has been altered genetically, it will most likely be of little or no use to the bee. Only a plant in its natural state is beneficial to bees. Some perennials that bees like are buttercups, clematis, hyacinth, rock cress, roses, sedum, cosmos, crocuses, dahlias, echinacea, English ivy, foxglove, geraniums, germander, globe thistle, hollyhocks, snowdrops, squills, tansy, and the gorgeous yellow hyssop.

Vegetable garden plants

There are some regular garden plants that bees love as well. The following common garden food plants are perfect for attracting bees: squash, wild garlic, cantaloupe, cucumbers, gourds, peppers, pumpkins, and watermelons, as well as a variety of berries such as blackberries, strawberries, and raspberries.

Many smaller plants are also great bee attractors. Herbs are often overlooked but should not be. They are another example of a plant that can work in your apiary and your kitchen. Herbs like the following are great for attracting bees to the garden: rosemary, mint, thyme, sage, bee balm, fennel, lavender, catnip, borage, coriander, and cilantro.

There are some larger trees and shrubs that are fantastic for attracting bees. These larger plants are wonderful for edging around your bee gardens and as barriers to hide your hives from prying eyes. Use shrubs and trees such as blueberry bushes, butterfly bush, buttonbush, honeysuckle, indigo, and privet. If you need a larger plant and have room for it to grow, try a few of these trees: basswood, black gum, black locus, alder, American holly, buckeyes, catalpa, and eastern redbud. Also, fruit trees are great, especially citrus and crabapples. You can also try golden rain tree, hawthorns, hazels, linden, magnolia, maples, mountain ash, sycamore, tulip, poplar, and willows.

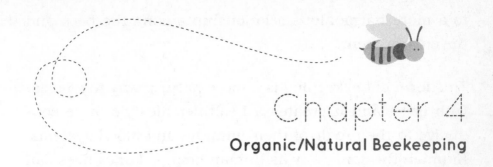

The notion of "going green" has affected every area of modern life. Anyone who has dealt with insects in their home or garden has been privy to their annoying characteristic of building a tolerance to any given chemical. Whatever product is being used stops working, and a more toxic product must then be used.

Beekeepers sometimes must face the varroa mite. It is usually treated by a poisonous chemical, but the destructive mites have shown signs of a growing resistance. Organic beekeepers take a different approach. Natural hive maintenance is a holistic alternative to the chemical treatments of modern beekeeping.

Many scientists and beekeepers believe that bees have been mistreated by beekeepers for so long that their immune systems and blood functions have been debilitated, making room for more diseases and pests like parasites to cause them harm. Organic beekeepers have turned to a more harmonious relationship among the bees and the environment.

This form of beekeeping is a more natural way to co-exist with bees, and it creates a healthier lifestyle more conducive to the repair of their immune and blood systems. In much the same way as human beings, honey bees can improve their health by removing the unhealthy factors from their environment.

The natural beekeeper extols the use of a positive attitude as an important beekeeping tool. Coming to the bee yard with a positive, fresh, and focused attitude makes a big difference in how the visit goes. Natural beekeepers believe in the philosophy that bees are like animals — they can sense fear, irritability, and stress, and they can react to it.

The idea behind successful organic beekeeping is to use the bee's natural tendencies, biological processes, and instinctive characteristic to help maintain a productive hive. Work with them instead of against them, as it were.

An important question to consider when deciding whether to make your beekeeping organic: What is the difference?

Chemicals found in normal farming activities make your product non-organic. But the manner in which your storage and harvesting is done is just as important as where your hives are located. *Organic* means all-natural growth without chemicals that would destroy the natural production of your final product.

In natural and organic beekeeping, *chemical* means it does not occur naturally in nature and is generated by human manipulation of chemical components. Everyone must decide how closely they will follow the guidelines of being *completely organic* in nature with respect to their beekeeping and honey production.

The downside of organic beekeeping is that honey output is not always at its highest level. The health and well-being of the bee is the top priority to the organic beekeeper. The focus is on quality as opposed to quantity.

Any beekeeper who plans to sell his or her honey and who has followed the natural ways of beekeeping still might not be able to label the honey as organic. This is because bees — as is their nature — forage wherever they please and may forage in gardens treated with pesticides. Some regulations require organic honey come from bees that have only foraged on an organic farm.

Backyard beekeepers, with a conscience toward respecting the needs of the honey bee, can make a difference and have a positive change in this balance. Farmers and the general public can also have a positive impact through making simple choices about when to spray or mow, as well as planting trees and flowers that provide valuable food for both domestic and feral bees.

Organic beekeeping practices include a variety of treatments that must use all-natural materials. These can be honey bee nutritional supplements, but there is a whole technique of specialized natural beekeeping tasks that encourage strong honey bees.

Many people think that bees are dangerous, and to some they can be deadly; however, honey bees are amazing, gentle creatures. They live in colonies that function as a single organism, with each honey bee working for the betterment of the entire colony. Their work pollinates the earth, helping the fauna of the planet while providing many useful goodies for mankind. But honey bees are also in dangerous decline, and we all need to become more aware of their plight. Though it may not seem important now, if the supply of honey becomes an issue of shortfall, it might be too late to change the amount of the damage we create in not being concerned.

Natural Beekeeping

Natural beekeeping and organic honey production go hand-in-hand for any natural beekeeper, but the latter is harder to accomplish. It is possible to keep your bees naturally and still not accomplish all of the requirements for the production and sale of organic honey.

Many natural beekeepers blame today's large-scale weakening of bee colonies on those beekeepers who do not apply natural beekeeping techniques. Most beekeepers, especially those who produce commercially, now use large amounts of what are considered dangerous chemicals to battle mites and other diseases. They also feed their colonies with artificial foods like syrups and supplements that make the production of honey from the honey bee less than all-natural. Those beekeepers are unable to label and sell their product as organic.

The source of honey and hive management are the two main aspects of natural beekeeping. Finding the best possible apiary location is an important part of natural beekeeping. Look for bee yards in protected areas close to water and flowering crops or wild flowers.

If honey is to be certified organic, the apiary must be placed in isolated locations that are several miles away from populated or industrialized zones and from farm fields that have been treated with chemicals and landfills. Organic honey producers cannot keep their colonies where a risk of corruption by any of the forbidden materials exists within a 4-mile radius of the hives. Finding an area that can be certified organic can be difficult. This explains why there are so few certified organic honeys on the market.

Other important factors

Be careful when choosing an apiary for organic beekeeping. Even in nature, there are numerous details to consider. It has been discovered that pine trees are capable of killing various microbes within a considerable distance of an apiary. It is also a known fact that feral bees that live in forests are usually healthy. If there is no forest in your area, you can plant some pine trees near your hives. These trees will also act as windbreakers.

Situate your hives so that when the sun rises, it shines on the front side and wakes your bees. This teaches your bees to become active early in the day and to get first dibs on the supply of nectar. During the hottest hours of the day, your hives should be shaded. Do not place apiaries near areas used by bears and other intruders.

Wet and warm air creates a perfect habitat for many types of bacteria. Although it is impossible to design an ideal beehive, especially for climates with frequent temperature changes, it is a goal worth pursuing. Improvements in ventilation would decrease hive humidity and reduce the need for beekeepers to intrude into bees' lives in order to help colonies to fight against bacteria. The fewer intrusions, the more productive our bees can be in producing the best possible product we could hope for — and an even larger quantity, as well.

The bees chosen for natural or organic beekeeping should be those that can survive the winter in your area and be able to get an early start in the spring, but organic beekeepers must breed their own queens.

Unless you have a trusted neighbor who can supply you with bees, many experts recommend purchasing a package from a large, reputable package supplier. Suppliers can be found in many areas of the country. For those who want a special strain of bee (such as one that is particularly mite-resistant), your best bet might still be to purchase a package from a supplier and promptly replace the queen. Most of the queen breeders who specialize in mite-resistant queens do not produce or sell packages. The queens cannot be clipped or use artificial insemination, and plastic hives cannot be used, though plastic can be used when packing the honey.

Pre-made wax foundation can also pose a problem for organic beekeepers. They can contain pesticide residues and non-organic feed (mainly corn syrup and sugar syrup) that create a less favorable product.

The extracting facilities must be inspected by federal food inspectors and, in order to get the organic label, a beekeeper must be certified by an official certifying organization. The requirements can vary by certifying organization and country. In some instances, a beekeeper must reside in a remote area — 4 miles or more in all directions from residential and agricultural areas.

But production per hive is likely to be much less in organic hives. Reports show the average organic production at 50 pounds per hive in 200 hives, compared with 150 pounds average in 1,300 conventional hives. Such differences are partly because of losses due to mites and partly a result of locations in remote areas with less productive forage.

It is worth it financially because certified-organic honey commands such a high price — sometimes three or four times higher than conventional honey.

Often, organic beekeepers will not use protective gear when opening the hive and going through the bees. Instead, they opt for going on the most advantageous days, staying focused, and making optimal use of the smoker.

Natural beekeepers will only use certain materials in their smokers. The gaseous products that begin combustion are replaced with dried and cured materials that are easily flammable on their own. They also choose to open the hive on the sunniest and warmest days, when more bees are away foraging. Many organic beekeepers do not find it necessary to use as much or any smoke on these days and, in fact, are not subjected to smoke at all.

Natural pest control

Before the creation of all the dangerous chemicals used in the control of pests and other harmful issues, essential oils were used to control pests in a natural way without creating a harmful climate. Plants produce many powerful chemicals, some of which are used to defend themselves against animals that eat plants as well as disease organisms. Natural essential oils are peppermint, clove, citrus, lavender, thyme, and rosemary oil. Certain combinations of these essential oils are effective and have low toxicity insecticides. Until recently, the availability of plant-based insecticides was limited to a few products such as neem oil and pyrethrum. Though these products are effective and exhibit low environmental impact, they have a limited range of uses.

To be a truly effective alternative to conventional insecticides, botanicals must be available in a range of formulations that can be used in a variety of pest-control situations. A pesticide formulation is simply the physical form of the product and the way in which it is applied. Dust, aerosol, liquid concentrate, and wettable powder formulations are all useful in different situations.

Be aware that not all pests are bad for the hive or organic honey production. Although wax moths do not kill healthy hives, they do eat what is left when a hive dies. Empty stored combs are unattractive to wax moths if they have never had brood in them. Wax moths avoid sunlight, are inactive in the cold, and are killed by hard freezing.

To manage foulbrood organically, it is important to inspect your hives regularly and promptly burn infected combs or equipment. In many locations, small hive beetles never cause enough trouble to even be noticed. If they should become a problem, try a cooking oil-based trap to drown them. This is a simple task of setting out containers of cooking oil with a small entrance near the hive. The beetles will go in but will be unable to get out.

Beekeepers who use excessive amounts of antibiotics are probably harming their bees as well as endangering other beekeepers. Honey bees have microorganisms in their digestive tracts that are negatively impacted by antibiotics. There are also resident bacteria and yeasts in the hive that are considered to be beneficial, e.g. those that help process pollen and nectar into bee bread. Excessive use of antibiotics selects the bacteria exposed for resistance to the antibiotic.

It has been strongly suggested that beekeepers learn to identify important bee pests (like American foulbrood and varroa mites) and carefully examine their hives on a regular basis. Problems recognized and properly treated early can generally be overcome without horrendous losses.

The organic payoff

Organic is the preferred choice for many of us when it comes to our foods, and honey is no exception. The requirements to deliver a truly organic honey are not easy to achieve and can become very costly. Honey can be a challenge to gather in non-organic climates. To create a truly organic product requires not only dedication to providing the best and most honest product possible, but also many resources and even more restrictions.

Can you imagine starting out in beekeeping with the plan to create only an organic honey product and what it would really entail? We know we would need to basically live in the middle of nowhere, on land that had never been used for production of crops or, at best, had not been used for the production of crops for at least the last ten years. We would need to have extensive knowledge of all-natural herbs to ensure we are using non-chemically based insecticides. We would need a good background in science and, more specifically, biochemistry. We would also need to have extensive knowledge of bees and their way of life.

Then there is the topic of crops and pollination. We would have to make sure there was enough of the right crops for the bees to use for pollination so that we would get the highest quality product possible.

Beekeeping as a hobby is a good way to start out, but be aware that it can grow to be an expensive and, at times, overwhelming task to get a product that is totally organic. For those who are seriously interested in creating the highest quality, naturally organic honey, it is an undertaking well worth the investment of time, research, and finances.

The eventual profit might take a while to see, but with so few true organic honey apiaries in the country, those who are willing to spend time studying, researching, and gathering information from the many beekeeping societies and experts could become pioneers in the field.

Once that is accomplished, however, you will have grown to love what you have most likely started as a hobby, and you can be proud to say you are one of the few truly organic honey producers.

So, here is to honey — pure, simple, sweet, and natural — a product not only of nature, but of a true desire to see something special develop that can make a real difference in the lives of those who dedicate their time to creating only the best product available.

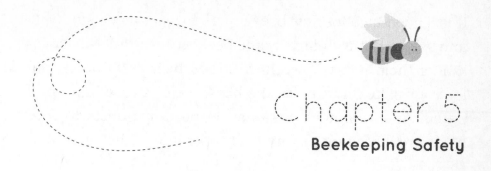

Beekeeping safety begins and ends with common sense, but getting stung by a bee is an inevitable part of the business. For those who find the prospect of learning about bees more intriguing than worrying about sustaining a few stings, this could be the start of a beautiful partnership.

New beekeepers should always wear beekeeping safety equipment. In fact, you should not visit your hive without wearing protective gear. Although your new bee colony is likely to be extremely gentle (especially during the first few weeks of the season), do not put yourself at risk.

As the colony grows and matures, there could be more than 60,000 bees present. The bees are often more curious than aggressive, and they love to explore dark holes, such as your ear canal and nostrils. Do not take any chances — wear a veil.

It is a good idea for new beekeepers to wear a bee suit, veil, and gloves to the apiary. Some beekeepers think the gloves hinder their ability to work with their bees and frames, but for your sake and that of the bees, come dressed and prepared. As a reminder, make sure that any guests to your hives are suited up as any beekeeper should be.

Bee Sting Remedies

The fact that bees bred for beekeeping are passive and not prone to stinging seldom does much to calm nervousness in people. It is possible to go for years without receiving a sting, and most stings are a result of a beekeeper's negligence. To keep sting incidents to a minimum, keep the following suggestions in mind:

- When working in the hive, move slowly and be calm. Do not make any sudden moves.

- Hold the frames firmly. Dropping a frame full of bees could result in being stung.

- Inspect the hive at the right time of day. Rainy weather and nighttime hours are not good.

- Do not wear dark colors; bees are attracted to them.

- Be clean and laundered, but not perfumed. Bees do not like body odor, but they do like flowery smells.

- Use a smoker, and always wear a veil and protective clothing.

- Do not swat. If bees are in the way, gently push them aside with a bee brush or soft flower.

As discussed earlier in Chapter 3, a bee sting is a stab with the stinger that injects a small dose of venom into the victim. Most people who are stung will have a small amount of redness, swelling, and moderate pain. Others have allergic reactions so severe that they have seizures, go into anaphylactic shock, or die.

The first thing to do if you are stung is to not panic. This is easier said than done, but running around or swatting at bees is an invitation for even more stings.

Second, smoke the area completely to mask the alarm pheromone that is released when a bee stings. When other bees smell that pheromone, it is a signal to attack.

Third, remove the stinger. Use your fingernail to scrape the stinger from your skin. The stinger is barbed and will remain in the skin, along with the bee's internal organs. It is important to scrape the stinger out; do not pinch or pull it because this squeezes the venom sac and injects more venom into the skin.

As soon as possible, apply a cold compress and take an antihistamine pill, or apply an antihistamine cream to help relieve much of the discomfort of swelling and itching.

There are a number of home remedies that long-time beekeepers swear by. These remedies may defy conventional wisdom, but they have been passed down to beekeepers for years. Antihistamines are the preferred medical technique for treating a bee sting, but here are a few other remedies that do not involve drugs. Though you may recognize some of these remedies as old wives' tales, they do work for relief; however, nothing will take the pain completely away:

- Apply honey
- Apply a tomato half
- Apply a small amount of vinegar
- Use a baking soda and water poultice
- Put ice on the site
- Use aloe vera gel or essential lavender oil
- Smear on a bit of mud
- Dab with egg yolk
- Rub on a wet aspirin

One important point to keep in mind is that getting stung actually helps build a tolerance to the bee venom, so with the next sting, the painful symptoms will not be as severe.

Before beginning your beekeeping adventure, be sure to consult your doctor. Ask your doctor if he or she feels it is in your best interest to get a prescription for an EpiPen. The EpiPen is an injection of epinephrine used immediately after a bee sting to prevent anaphylactic shock. Anaphylaxis (or anaphylactic shock) is a potentially life-threatening allergic reaction. Symptoms include difficulty breathing or swallowing, hives, or swelling around the mouth or eyes. Although this may be successfully treated with epinephrine, in the event you ever have to use an EpiPen, it is imperative that you are seen by a doctor for follow-up diagnosis and care.

Chapter 6
The Business of Bees

There is an old beekeeping joke that goes something like: Sure, there is a lot of money flowing in the honey business — it flows right out of your pocket. Though it is true that most people keep bees for the pure enjoyment of the activity, there are a select few who are beekeepers for the earning potential. Not everyone takes their beekeeping down this route, but all beekeepers should be familiar with the aspects of the business end.

There is the chance your bees could produce lots of honey — even more than you can use. Why not sell it? There is also the chance that you will accidentally stumble upon a great honey body lotion recipe while playing around in the kitchen. Sell it, become successful, and earn a substantial income; it is possible. *See more on products you can produce and sell with your beekeeping in Chapter 7.* Business of any kind takes knowledge and experience to succeed, but also a certain amount of luck and timing. Even if you do not decide to make a small business out of your beekeeping hobby, you should understand the basics of how to run one. This chapter will walk you through the steps to success.

Steps to Success

The following six factors are essential to the long-term success of any business:

1. Passion is the prime ingredient. A successful business is more than just a business to its owner.

2. A solid business foundation is built on a well-considered, strategic plan.

3. Excellent customer relations are the hallmark of success.

4. Quality, reliability, and service are emphasized.

5. Procedures, products, pricing, and all the strategic necessities of the business are regularly evaluated and monitored by the owner.

6. A flexible business remains successful as it adapts readily to changes in the industry, technology, and market.

Almost everyone has dreamed of owning his or her own business. Oftentimes, these dreams are the result of dealing with difficult bosses, low pay, long hours, swing shifts, and other frustrations that come from working for someone else. In the safe confines of the imagination, the vision of owning a business is immensely satisfying: You are your own boss, you make your own decisions, and you do not have to answer to anyone else. What could be better?

While there are elements of truth in this dream-world vision of business ownership, it is also true that in reality, business owners have problems, too. The problems are different from the frustrations faced by employees, but they are serious and stomach-wrenching just the same. You will want to know your personal capacity to deal with the problems of business ownership before you jump out of the workforce and take over the boss's chair.

If you plan to start your business from scratch, you are on your own; however, your costs are lower, and you will not have to follow the plans and policies of a franchise, or deal with the reputation of a previous business owner. You will be in complete control and will have the prospect of success or failure on your shoulders. It will be up to you to find customers, market your services, research your vendors and potential partners, hire any employees, and set up your office. This is a huge challenge, but if you have a vision in mind, you may be eager to take it on. Remember — planning is key.

Author's Apiary

Beekeeping College 101

What is Beekeeping College? Well, it is basically getting your Ph.D. in beekeeping without going back to college. It is a five-year program designed to provide a concentrated educational track to teach beekeepers all there is to know about honey bees. There are four levels of advancement. Level names and requirements may vary from state to state, but overall the programs are very similar and have the same goal. Even beekeepers with 30 years of experience have to begin at the first level.

Apprentice Beekeeper: Be a registered beekeeper for at least one year; pass written and practical exams.

Advance Beekeeper: Hold the rank of Apprentice Beekeeper for at least one year; pass six training modules; pass written and practical exams; perform five community service credits.

Master Beekeeper: Hold the rank of Apprentice and Advance Beekeeper for one year each; perform 10 community service credits; demonstrate expertise in several subspecialties; choose a major in a subcategory; pass a written exam.

Master Craftsman Beekeeper: Hold the rank of Master Beekeeper for at least two years; perform 15 public service credits; demonstrate expertise in communication skills; satisfy major requirements; pass a written exam.

Develop a Business Plan

If the previous section got you thinking about the what-ifs of starting your own business, you may want to sketch out a business plan. The only way you can reach your goal of succeeding with your business is by having a plan. It is difficult at best to establish and operate a business when you do not quite know how to go about it — let alone to try to accomplish it without a thorough assessment of what you want to accomplish, how you plan to go about it, and what financial support you have to accomplish it. As you prepare to undertake the enormous task of starting a new business, evaluate your situation as it stands today and visualize where you want to be three to five years from now. To work your way from today's standpoint to owning and operating a successful bee-related business, you must set yourself goals to reach along the way that will serve as benchmarks on your road to success.

The most important and basic information to include in a business plan include:

- State your business goals.

- Describe the approach you will take to accomplish those goals.

- Discuss what potential problems you may encounter along the way and how you plan to address those problems.

- Outline the organizational structure of the business (as it is today and how you plan it to be).

- State the capital you will need to get it started and to keep it in operation.

There are various formats and models available for developing business plans. There are even entire books devoted to guiding you through the development of a business plan. However, before you constrain yourself to any one business plan format, take into consideration that business plans should be as unique as the business for which it is being written. No two businesses are the same, and even though there may be some basic similarities, each business is as individual and unique as people. Therefore, even though it is recommended that you follow the basic structure of commonly used templates, you should customize your business plan to fit your bee-related needs. There are a number of Web sites that provide you with a variety of samples and templates that can also be used as reference, such as **www.bplans.com**, **www.nebs.com/nebsEcat/business_tools/bptemplate**, and **www.planmagic.com**. You can also use **http://honeybeesbeekeeping.wikispaces.com/Beekeeping+Business+Plan** and **www.buzzle.com/articles/beekeeping-business.html**.

When writing your business plan, stay focused on its ultimate purpose and take into consideration the many reasons why the plan is developed and its possible applications. For instance, if you do not have a loan proposal — essentially a condensed version of the business plan and used by businesses to request financing — when trying to secure financing for your business, business plans are great supporting documentation to attach to a loan application. Plans are also used as a means of introducing your business to a new market or presenting your business to a prospective business partner or investor. Look at the following template for gaining an idea of what your business plan can look like, which follows the basic structure of a generic plan and incorporates key elements of a business.

Parts of a business plan

Cover page

The cover page should be evenly laid out with all the information centered on the page. Always write the name of your company in all-capital letters in the upper half of the page. Several line spaces down, write the title "Business Plan." Last, write your company's address, the contact person's name (your name), and the current date.

NAME OF COMPANY

Business Plan

Address
Contact Name
Date

Table of Contents

Mission Statement

   I. Executive Summary

   II. Description of Proposed Business

   III. Management and Staffing

   IV. Market Analysis

      a. Industry background

b. *Target market*

c. *Product description*

d. *Market approach strategy*

V. Marketing Strategy

VI. Operations

VII. Financial Projections

VIII. Conclusion

IX. Supporting Documents

Body of the Business Plan

MISSION STATEMENT

When writing your mission statement, three key elements that must be taken into consideration and discussed are the purpose of your business, the goods or services that you provide, and a statement as to your company's attitude toward your employees and customers. A well-written mission statement could be as short as one paragraph but should not be longer than two.

I. EXECUTIVE SUMMARY

The executive summary should be about one to two pages in length and should actually be written last, as it is a summary of all the information you would have included in the plan. It should address what your market is, the purpose of the business, where will it be located, and how it will be managed. It is a good idea to discuss the various elements of your business plan in the order you address them in the rest of the document.

II. DESCRIPTION OF PROPOSED BUSINESS

Describe in detail the purpose for which the business plan is being written. State what you intend to accomplish. Describe your goods, services, and the role your business will play in the overall global market. Explain what makes your business different from all the rest in the same arena. Clearly identify the goals and objectives of your business.

III. MANAGEMENT AND STAFFING

State whom the owners of the business are, as well as other key employees with backgrounds in the international trade industry. Identify the management talent you have on board (this may even include yourself), as well as any others you may need in the future to expand your business. For instance, it may just be yourself when starting up; however, in your plans for expansion, you might think about incorporating someone well-versed in the business of beekeeping and production of bee products. The management and staffing section of the plan could be as short as one paragraph, if you are the only employee, or it could be as long as a page or two, depending on how many people you have and anticipate having as part of your staff.

IV. MARKET ANALYSIS

If you are new to the industry, do your research and include information that you have acquired through research and data collection. There are numerous sources of information available, both online and through printed media. This process will add validity to your presentation, and you will be better prepared to answer any questions that may be presented to you. Essential elements to include in this section a description of your products or services, identify your competition, and identify what your planned strategy and approaches are to the market.

Target Market

This is one of the largest sections of the business plan because you will be addressing key issues that will determine the volume of sales and, ultimately, the revenue that you will be able to generate for your business. Identify the characteristics of the principal market you intend to target, such as demographics, market trends, and geographic location of the market.

Discuss what resources you used to find the information you needed on your target market. Elaborate on the size of your primary target market — your potential customers — by indicating the possible number of prospective customers, what their purchasing tendencies are in relation to the product or services you anticipate providing, their geographical location, and the forecasted market growth for that particular market segment. Expand your discussion to include the avenues you will use to reach your market. Include whether you plan to use the Internet, printed media, trade shows, and such. Explain the reasons why you feel confident that your company will be able to effectively compete in such a vast industry.

Product Description

Do not just describe your product or service — describe it as it will benefit or fill the needs of potential customers, and center your attention on where you have a clear advantage. Elaborate on what your products or services are.

V. MARKETING STRATEGY

In order to operate a financially successful business, you must not only maintain a constant flow of income, but also boost your profits by increased sales. The marketing strategy element of the business plan identifies your current and potential customers, as well as the means you will use to advertise your business directly to them. For a large, well-established business, it would probably be more appropriate to prepare a separate marketing strategy plan; however, for the start-up company, it would be appropriate to include the marketing strategy plan as part of the business plan. Even as part of the business plan, the marketing strategy section should include the following elements: products and services, pricing strategy, sales/distribution plan, and advertising/promotions plan.

Products and Services

Describe in detail the services your business provides, how the services are provided, and what makes the services that you provide unique and different from other businesses in the industry that provide the same service or deal with the same goods. Address the benefits of using your services or buying your goods instead of those of the competitors.

Pricing Strategy

You will be better off making a reasonable profit rather than pricing yourself out of the market and losing money by pricing your goods or services too high. Therefore, you must take extreme care when pricing your goods and services. The most effective method of doing this is by gauging your costs, estimating the tangible benefits to your customers, and making a comparison of your goods, services, and prices to similar ones on the market. A good rule of thumb to follow is to set your price by taking into consideration how much the goods or services cost you, then add what you think would be a fair price for the benefits the goods or services will provide to the end customer.

Sales and Distribution

Now that you have determined how to price your goods and services, it is time to think about how you are going to sell and distribute your products and services. Describe the system you will use for processing orders, shipping the goods, and billing your customers. Also, address what methods of payment will be acceptable from your customers, including credit terms and discounts. In regard to the actual distribution of the goods, discuss the methods of distribution you anticipate using, as well as the anticipated costs associated with it. There are several methods of distribution to choose from, such as direct mail, telemarketing, wholesale outlets, retail stores, or via a Web site on the Internet.

Advertising and Promotion

Discuss how you plan to advertise your products and services through market-specific channels. One of your goals is to break down what percentage of your advertising budget will be spent in which media. For instance, the cost of advertising through normal channels and via the Internet differ significantly, and the return on your investment on each may not be worth what you spent.

VI. OPERATIONS

Concentrate your discussion on how to improve resources in operations and production, which will facilitate the success of the company. Discuss the business's current and proposed location, describing in detail any existing facilities.

VII. FINANCIAL PROJECTIONS

When developing your financial projections, you must take into consideration every possible expense, expected and unexpected, yet be conservative in your revenues. It is not critical that your actual revenues exceed the estimated amount; however, it is not a good situation when expenses are more than expected. Your projections should be addressed for the next three to five years, breaking down each year with the following information: forecasted income statements, cash flow statements, balance sheets, and capital expenditure budgets.

VIII. CONCLUSION

The conclusion is the last written element of the business plan. Make use of this last opportunity to state your case wisely, highlighting key issues discussed in the plan. Then, wrap it up and close with a summary of your future plans for the expansion and progress of your business. Use language that will help the reader visualize what you will be able to accomplish and how successful your business will be, should you receive the support you are requesting.

IX. SUPPORTING DOCUMENTS

Attaching supporting documentation to your business plan will certainly strengthen it and make it more valuable. However, do not over-burden it with too many attachments; finding a balance is important. Before you start attaching documents, ask yourself if that particular piece of information will make a difference — if the answer is no, then leave it out. Documents that you should attach include:

- Copies of the business principals' résumés

- Tax returns and personal financial statements of the principals for the last three years

- A copy of licenses, certifications, and other relevant legal documents

- A copy of the lease or purchase agreement, if you are leasing or buying space

- Copies of letters of intent from suppliers (if applicable)

Author's Apiary

You bee the judge: Evaluating honey for competition

What if you were able to wear a terrific white smock and matching hat, have fun, and add that you are a Certified Welsh Honey Judge to your résumé? Universities and institutes, such as the University of Florida and the YHC/UGA Bee-keeping Institute in Georgia, have partnered with the Welsh Bee-keepers' Association in England to offer training and certification to become a honey show judge. Contact your state beekeepers' association to see if a certification program is offered in your area of the state. From start to finish, the certification process takes a minimum of one year — it takes longer depending on your ability to complete the documented experience required. The Welsh Honey Judge certification process involves:

(1) Attending an initial training class,

(2) Writing a documented experience as a judge's assistant,

(3) Writing a documented experience as a honey show judge, and

(4) Completing an oral examination successfully.

The purchase of an official judge's smock and hat is required prior to taking your exam, and when you are serving as a judge or steward, you are expected to wear your official outfit in respect of the high standards of professionalism the certification carries. What you will have in the end is not only an extensive knowl-edge of honey, but also the ability to be called upon to be a certified honey judge anywhere in the world.

Keeping Records

Record keeping for a beekeeping business is similar to keeping records for any other small business. Everything from expenses and profits to stock inventory and physical characteristics must be recorded. Some beekeepers prefer the latest bookkeeping computer software, while others may simply place stones strategically on top of the hives to distinguish which ones have been checked and which ones have honey. What is important is to choose a system that is easy to navigate and comprehend.

The most efficient way for new beekeepers to keep records is with a daily log. Each hive inspection should have an entry that includes the state of the hive, the date and time visited, general hive observations, and inspection notes.

Another important aspect of record keeping involves the honey harvest. Be sure to note the percent of capped cells and the physical characteristics of the honey, such as color and thickness. Note the number of frames replaced along with the date and location, and even the taste and flavor of the honey. Each season can bring a slightly different taste based on the flowering vegetation at the time.

As a general guide, try to answer these questions during each hive visit:

- Are there any signs of illness or disease?

- Are there more brood frames than there were at the last inspection?

- Is the queen present and healthy?

- Is there enough room for hive life to prosper until the next inspection?

- Are there any signs of impending swarming?

- Are there enough honey supers to suffice until the next inspection?

If there is more than one colony, compare notes for each. Comparisons can show if a colony is acting peculiar, and this also may alert you to the first signs of disease, pest infestation, or illness.

Create a bio sheet for each colony. This offers specifics for every colony, such as temperament, quality of cappings and comb, honey crop, brood pattern, and pollen storage. This kind of information is essential for selective breeding. Some beekeepers will breed for strong brood traits or large honey crops.

A separate record detailing just the queen's information is necessary. A queen is usually replaced every two years. With up-to-date records and detailed notes on the queen's behavior and accomplishments throughout the months, it will be easier to determine the replacement cycle.

If you are a member of a beekeepers' association in your community, you may have the opportunity to purchase an insurance policy that can protect you against lost bees and destroyed hives. You can also get coverage for loss of equipment, bee food, and even your honey. You can get full coverage on your entire honey harvest against problems that can occur during transport, flood, fire, vandalism, and damages due to pesticides and herbicides.

Another perk is in accidental death and dismemberment policies that beekeepers, their families, and employees can take out in case of a tragedy while beekeeping. This can be include anything from fires to allergic reactions to stings. You can also apply for reimbursement for legal fees and opinions in the case you win. Make sure you know the full terms of any insurance policy you take out concerning your beekeeping business. Take the time to familiarize yourself with all your rights and responsibilities, as well as the benefits you will receive.

Taxes will also be an issue for you at some point. Beekeeping is considered an agricultural business, and you are therefore required to pay taxes on any and all monies received from the sale of bees, honey, wax, and other products. There are no tax credits available just for beekeepers, but there are many for farmers on the federal and local levels. You can take advantage of some of these as a beekeeper.

There are many avenues to pursue when it comes to taxes for beekeepers. However, it is a wide misconception that you do not have to incorporate your beekeeping business to receive the best tax credits. The U.S. Department of Agriculture considers bees as livestock, just the same as cattle or pigs. Most states do not charge a sales tax for items purchased for farming or, in our case, beekeeping.

Because many state laws differ, and each beekeeper's case and situation is different, your best bet is to acquire the help of a certified public accountant (CPA) to help with taxes. Most CPAs will charge between $250 and $500 a year to help prepare your taxes for your beekeeping business. They will save you at least that much as well as immeasurable time and aggravation trying to fill out the paperwork.

CASE STUDY: BEEKEEPING
SUCCESS — TIPS FROM A
BACKYARD BEEKEEPER

Howland Blackiston
Beekeeper

Beekeepers must learn how to tend to their hives. Without proper hive maintenance, all kinds of problem (starvation, disease, pests, etc.) can arise, but when a beekeeper is educated and diligent, problems will be minimal.

One of the most basic and important skills that a beekeeper must learn is how to identify eggs. It is not an easy task because the eggs are translucent white and tiny — only about 1.7 millimeters long. But finding eggs is one of the surest ways to confirm that your queen is alive. It is a skill that every beekeeper will use just about every time they visit their hives. Eggs are often easier to spot on a sunny day. Hold the comb at a slight angle and, with the sun shining over your shoulder, illuminate the deep recesses of the cell.

"I recommend investing in an inexpensive pair of reading glasses," Blackiston said. "The magnification can really help you spot the eggs, even if you do not normally need reading glasses. Once you discover your first egg, it will be easier to know what you are looking for during future inspections.

"The best time of year to begin beekeeping depends upon where you live. A good time to start is a few months before the 'official' launch of the season, when the flowers come into bloom."

In the United States, the season officially starts in early spring when the bee breeders in the southern states have packaged their bees to sell. It is important not to wait until the last minute. Use the winter months to assemble your equipment, research bees and beekeeping, and order your bees for a spring delivery. First-time beekeepers should consider joining a bee club in their area. This is a great way to learn more about beekeeping and meet new friends. Many clubs have special programs for new beekeepers (called new bees) and hands-on workshops. New beekeepers might also consider asking an experienced beekeeper to become their mentor — someone who can answer questions and who can help them get started the right way.

The best time to install your bees is in early April or May. Spring varies from state to state, but try to time your start to coincide with the first early-season blossoms, and a few weeks prior to the fruit bloom. Do not wait until June or July; starting a hive in summer will not give your colony a chance to get strong for the winter.

In the northern states that experience winter, bees need 60 to 70 pounds of capped honey to survive. This is equal to 10 deep frames of capped honey. Always leave this much for your bees during winter; unless your winters are short. Anything above this can be harvested.

The brood cells are capped with tan or brown porous wax and the capping is slightly convex. Honey cells are capped with white, air-tight wax, and the capping is flat, not convex. Bees can survive on the sugar water for a short time, but they need both carbohydrates and protein. The sugar water (or honey) provides the carbohydrates, and the protein from pollen. Sugar water is typically only fed to the bees in the spring and fall — not all season.

The smoker is a beekeepers' best friend. Smoke calms the bees and allows for safe inspection of the hives. The smoker is a fire chamber with bellows designed to produce a lot of smoke. Learn how to light it so that it stays lit, and never overdo the smoking process — a little goes a long way.

"Never inspecting a hive is probably the biggest no-no of beekeeping," Blackiston said. "I have seen so many folks go the whole season without ever looking in on their hives. This is a surefire recipe for trouble. These lethargic people are 'bee-havers,' not 'beekeepers.'"

Careful and diligent management and routine inspections are the best practices when it comes to keeping disease and pests away. Know what to look for, and learn the visual signs of trouble.

New beekeepers should always wear beekeeping safety equipment. Do not visit your hive without wearing a veil. Although your new bee colony is likely to be extremely gentle (especially during the first few weeks of the season), do not put yourself at risk.

"Many new beekeepers prefer to use gloves during installation and routine inspections," Blackiston said. "I discourage this practice, especially with a new colony or early in the season, because gloves can inhibit a beekeeper's sense of touch, which can result in inadvertent injury to the bees. That is counterproductive and only makes them more defensive when they see you coming."

It is possible that a colony can exist without drones in the winter. Once the weather gets cooler and the mating season comes to a close, the worker bees will not tolerate having drones around. After all, those fellows have big appetites and would consume a tremendous amount of food during the winter. So, in cooler climates and at the end of the nectar-producing season, the worker bees systematically expel the drones from the hive; this is a signal that the beekeeping season is over for the year.

One of the biggest errors made in beekeeping is when a new queen is introduced to a colony when an old queen is still alive. As long as there is an old queen in the hive, a new queen will not be accepted.

I have seen many new beekeepers claim they have no queen when, in fact, they do. Then they wonder why the new queen they introduced was killed.

A backyard beekeeper since 1984, Howland Blackiston is the author of the best-selling book Beekeeping for Dummies *(John Wiley & Sons). Blackiston has written dozens of articles about beekeeping and appeared on several television and radio programs, including The Discovery Channel, CNBC, CNN, NPR, Sirius Satellite Radio, and regional shows, and has been a keynote speaker at conferences in more than 40 countries. Blackiston is the founder of* **www.bee-commerce.com**, *an Internet-based store that sells beekeeping supplies and equipment for the backyard beekeeper. He is the past president of Connecticut's Backyard Beekeepers Association, one of the nation's largest (nearly 400* *members) regional clubs for the hobbyist beekeeper. Blackiston and his wife, Joy, live in Weston, Connecticut.*

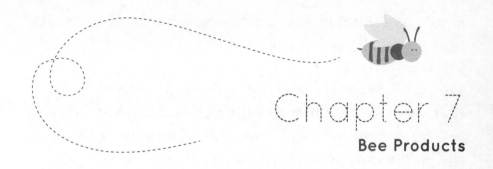

f sitting in the sun on a nice comfortable chair, sipping iced tea, and watching your bees busy at work is not the only enjoyment you want to get from being a beekeeper, then there are plenty of productive things to do to keep you as busy as your bees. Processing honey, forming wax, packaging propolis and larvae, dipping candles, making cosmetics, and working in the world of apitherapy will fill your days with both fun and profit.

Selling Honey

Honey is most often sold by the pound, with prices ranging from $6 - $8 a pound. It is usually sold in plastic or glass containers. Glass has a certain classy look to it, but plastic is durable.

The label should contain pertinent information, such as company name, ordering details, and ingredients. The National Honey Board organization's Web site (**www.honey.**

com) has printable labels, advertisements, and fliers available free of charge.

Proper fill is to just about the circle in the neck of the jar, so that when one holds a jar of honey and looks straight on, one cannot see through; there should be no space between the jar lid and the honey-fill line.

According to veteran beekeeper Lynda Cook Rizzardi, one of the best phrases that some beekeepers use in packaging is, "Do neither over-fill nor under-fill a jar of marketable honey. If you over-fill, you are cheating yourself; if you under-fill, you are cheating the customer."

Cost of honey and honey products might seem expensive to some buyers, but it is your honey, and it is your price. Remember that the beekeeper has purchased the bees, possibly a new queen, the hive body, frames, foundation, supers and spacers, and any other needed supplies. He or she has also personally checked the progress of the work in the hive, removed supers for packaging and processing, cut the comb and extracted the honey, jarred the honey, labeled, and done all the preparation to distribute or show the product. The bees do not do all the work.

Show honey

Honey entered in competition is known as show honey. Competition exists at state, national, and even international levels. Other bee products that can be judged include cuts of honeycomb, honey frames, beeswax, and honey bees.

Most competitions will have similar criteria to judge the honey for awards. Cleanliness is absolutely crucial. There should be no debris or foreign matter — bee wings, body parts, hairs, dirt, dust, lint, or particles of any kind — in a jar of honey.

The color and flavor of show honey is dependent upon the major blooms in season during the honey flow. Different flowering trees, shrubs, and flowers provide color and flavor. If a beekeeper is fortunate enough to have different colors and flavors of honey, it is best to keep these separated for judging and selling purposes. Both experienced and new beekeepers quickly learn that customers want a variety of honey flavors and products. Some beekeepers will mix everything they remove from the hive and have a blended, neutral color and flavor.

There are five color divisions for the comb or chunk honey entries, including white, extra light amber, light amber, amber, and dark amber. Criteria for these entries generally include cleanliness, accuracy of fill, absence of crystals, flavor, and container appearance. The comb honey is also judged on neatness and uniformity of the cut comb, the absence of water, cappings, uncapped cells, and pollen.

The cut refers to the honeycomb. The entire comb should be cut at one time. Cut the comb so that it will reach to the neck of the jar. When filling with the extracted honey, try to keep the cut comb centered in the jar. Once the jar is filled, take a thin-bladed knife and remove any of the wax capping that may float to the top.

Honey frame entries may be entered using deep, medium, or shallow frames, generally in either a light or dark category. The judge will look for uniformity of appearance, absence of uncapped cells' cleanliness, absence of travel stains across the comb surface, uniformity of color and comb draw, and freedom of granulation and pollen.

Beeswax entries are divided into several categories: a molded piece of wax, weighing a minimum amount; a novelty piece of wax; candles; or products of wax (furniture polish, lip gloss, lotions, and creams). A judge will look for cleanliness, uniformity of appearance, and color. A nice lemon-yellow color is considered the standard in judging the wax alone. Also noted are aroma, absence of cracks and shrinkage, the skills involved, and the design.

Honey bees should be viewed from a special observation box. The observation hive must contain a frame of brood, a frame of honey, and a marked queen bee. The judge will look at the comb in both frames to see if it is even in appearance and color; look at the brood pattern in the brood frame; check the rate of worker cells in the brood frame; examine the sufficiency of the laying queen; and check the conformity of the bees to the species specified on the entry tag.

Using wax

Wax is a big part of any beekeeper's business. There are many product ideas, from candles to cosmetics, that might appeal to the newcomer.

Most beekeepers make their candles from the wax cappings of honey cells. This is the lightest colored wax. Wax is white when it is first made, but it quickly changes with exposure to honey and pollen. The actual comb can be used as well but melts down to a much darker color.

To prepare the wax, begin by soaking the well-strained cappings water overnight. The next day, drain the cups and place in an enamel, ceramic, or stainless-steel pot. An old coffee pot works well. Never use aluminum or iron because it stains and discolors the wax. Heat the pot in a double boiler. Never heat directly over the actual flame or heat source because wax is extremely flammable. Use an electric heat source instead of gas or another open flame fuel. If no double boiler is available, fill a larger pot with water and insert the pot with the wax over the hot water. Be careful not to let the water boil. If water gets into your wax, it causes imperfections and sputtering in candles. Never leave the room when melting wax.

Once the wax is thoroughly melted, pour it through a filter. A double layer of paper towels works well for small quantities of wax. These paper towels are great to save for use in lighting the smoker when opening the hive and working with the bees. After the wax is completely filtered, set it aside to cool.

Cleaning the wax is important for strong-burning candles with little smoke. The easiest way may be to melt it in a pan of water. Wax is light and will float, and all the impurities will sink. Heat the water. As the wax melts, ladle it off the surface and put it in a clean plastic container.

Take small chunks of the cooled wax and re-melt them in a double boiler or over a pan of boiling water. After melting, filter again — but this time, filter through a piece of clean cloth. Stretch the cloth over a metal coffee tin and secure with a rubber band. Leave just enough slack in the cloth to form a slight dip for the wax to sit in as it drips through the filter.

This second filtering is also important. The more finely the wax is filtered, the better your candle products. After this last filtering, put the clean wax into a milk carton. The wax cools inside and, when hardened, can easily be removed.

Author's Apiary

Beeswax: The multi-purpose wonder

We have discussed some great uses for beeswax, but there are many more. It is also used in dentistry, blacksmithing, and in cartoon animation. Here are some other fascinating uses from beekeeper Lawrence Cutts. Beeswax can be used to:

- Rub on your iron for smoother ironing
- Rub on screws and nails for smoother driving
- Lubricate ammunition
- Rub on thread to make for easier needle threading, sewing, and tangle-preventing
- Lubricate doors, windows, drawers, and zippers
- Wax your mustache or eyebrows
- Wax bow strings
- Wax leather straps
- Wax fly lines and use in fly tying
- Make a good furniture polish when mixed with linseed oil
- Waterproof leather boots
- Rub on pie pans, cake pans, and cookie sheets to prevent sticking
- Lubricate water skis, snow skis, sleds and toboggans
- Make a good wood preserver when mixed with mineral oil or turpentine
- Help camouflage odor on traps
- Remove pinfeathers from poultry and other fowl
- Wax braces on teeth
- Lubricate band saw blades when cutting aluminum
- Polish gemstones

Candle making

Even the hobbyist beekeeper might be inspired to indulge in the art of candle making. Some will make an entire business of their handmade beeswax candles and, of course, their other products. Beeswax makes the best candles because it retains its form, smells better, and burns slowly with less smoke. For the beekeeper who is considering making candles for fun or profit, beeswax can be heated and poured into molds, rolled, or dipped.

Dipping candles is one of oldest technique of candle making. It is by far the most difficult, but worth the time and effort if your plan is to sell in bulk. To get started, dip a wax-coated wick into a tall double boiler of melted wax. Dip the wick, wait one to two minutes, and dip again. Repeat this process. Each time the candle is dipped, a small layer is left on the wick. After the candles have dried — but are not too hard — slice the end with a sharp knife to give it a flat end.

Poured candles can be bigger and stronger than dipped candles. Hang the wick over a ceramic bowl or pie plate to catch the wax. Pour the hot wax over the wick, slowly twisting the wick to ensure total coverage. Lean the wick over a prop and let dry. Repeat as many times as needed. Temperature is important here: If your wax is too cold, it will stop before it gets to the bottom of the wick and not cover smoothly. If it is too hot, it will run to the bottom of the holding container, and not enough will stick to the wax.

Roll the candle on a countertop or between two sheets of glass or plastic to straighten. Cut the nut or bolt from the wick and trim the ends of the candle to an even edge.

Maybe your dream is to make holiday-themed or religious-shaped candles. Molded candles can take the shape of anything. Get a bucket full of sand for this procedure; insert the closed mold into the sand to keep it upright and to protect any surfaces from spilled wax.

Be sure the metal molds are warmed to room temperature. Coat the inside of the mold with a cooking oil spray or a liquid detergent. Use a paint brush; make sure to get the oil or detergent in every nook and cranny. Do not leave any air bubbles, because they cause imperfections in the candle surface. Let the molds sit overnight. Add a light dusting of talcum powder to help prepare them for wax pouring.

Insert the wick into the mold, pulling it out at least 2 inches on the underside. Tie that end around a bobby pin, toothpick, or something else to hold secure and keep the wick from slipping back into the opening of the mold.

Clamp the mold together and insert in the pan of sand until snug. Fill the mold from the open hole at the top. Let cool several hours, then fill in any shrinkage that has occurred. Beeswax loses a considerable amount of mass as it solidifies from liquid form. The bigger the mold, the more shrinkage will occur. Fill the candle again as it dries. Allow to cool slowly. Fast cooling of beeswax results in warping and weak candles with cracks and distortions. Wrap in newspaper and put in a cool, dry place for 24 hours.

When unmolding your candle, patience is the key. Loosen any clamps and slowly pry apart your mold. If your molds are metal mold and are being difficult to remove, try putting them in the freezer for 15 minutes, then give them a sharp tap with the butt of a knife.

Place candles on newspaper and allow them to air dry. Wrap them in tissue paper and store in an airtight container. After several days, a whitish bloom will cover the candle. No worries — this is normal and only has to be buffed away with a cloth.

Show wax

Wax can be shown at local county and state fairs as well as contests all over the world. Wax contests have their own criteria for judging such as purity of the wax, color, and weight. It can be judged in blocks of pure, natural wax, candles, cosmetics, and household goods like furniture polish. Contact your local agricultural division for information on local contests.

Cosmetics

Beeswax is a great protectant for the skin. It has emollient properties as well as soothing and softening characteristics that help the skin retain moisture. It is used in cosmetic as a thickening agent, emulsifier (a mixture used in makeup to keep surfaces smooth and liquids dispersed), and humectant (a substance used in makeup to absorb water). When mixed with oils, butters, and other natural ingredients, it becomes a gentle addition to the medicine cabinet.

Beeswax cosmetics, like Burt's Bees® products, are fairly easy to make at home. To get started, gather a few items such as extra virgin olive oil, a scented essential oil, and beeswax.

Try making a simple lip cream by mixing one part beeswax to four parts extra virgin olive oil. Melt the wax and oil together in a double boiler. Once the wax mixture is at the right consistency, let it cool and add a few drops of an essential oil like peppermint or spearmint. When the mixture is almost cool, pour it into small containers.

Hand creams are a bit looser in consistency. To make a hand cream, simply use more olive oil. Start with a mixture of one part beeswax to six parts olive oil. Mix the same way as the lip cream. Melt the wax in a double boiler, or put the wax into a pot and place that pot into a larger pot of boiling water. Melt the wax slowly and stir in the olive oil until it is completely mixed together with a smooth consistency. Remove the mixture from the heat and add in the essential oil of your choice. Try rose or lavender.

Bee Larvae

The larvae of honey bees are highly sought-after commodities, and in many parts of the world it is considered a delicacy. In China it often appears on restaurant menus, and in Vietnam it is possible to eat the larvae straight from the hive.

Bee larvae must be fresh for consumption, so it is important to have a buyer already lined up. Check the monthly newsletters and beekeepers publications for ads from companies looking to buy larvae and other bee products. Larvae can be sold fresh and powdered, and the bees must be free of disease and pests.

Check the state and federal laws before shipping products overseas and before purchasing any bee larvae.

Apitherapy

Apitherapy is the practice of using bee products for medicinal purposes and to promote healthy living and healing. It can be any bee product, like venom, honey, wax, propolis, or royal jelly. Apitherapy is used for the treatment of illnesses and health issues like gout, shingles, burns and cuts, multiple sclerosis, tendonitis, and other various wounds and infections.

Honey can be used as a dressing for burns, cuts, and scrapes. It is highly antibacterial and can help to keep wounds sterile and heal them faster.

Royal jelly is the food that bees produce for themselves and their brood. It is used in some cosmetics and touted for its revitalizing properties. You can even get royal jelly in capsule form and use it to aid in the treatment of many illnesses.

There are some beekeepers who will harvest the pollen from bees as they enter the hive. Pollen can be used to alleviate allergy symptoms and build up a resistance to other allergens.

Propolis is used for several medicinal reasons and health issues. It is very antibacterial and found in many thera-peutic and cosmetic creams.

Bee Venom

Bee venom is not just a poison — there are many useful functions for this deadly natural concoction, as well. Sell-ing bee venom is a valuable part of many a beekeeper's business but should be handled with care. A lethal dose for an adult human is considered to be 2.8 milligrams of venom per kilogram of body weight. For example, a person weighing 60 kg (132 pounds) has a 50 percent chance of surviving injections totaling 168 mg of bee venom.

Bees were used for medicinal purposes dating back to ancient times. Egyptians treated ailments and diseases with ointments made from bees. Writings from over 2,000 years ago show that the Chinese used it as well. Even Hip-pocrates mentions bee stings in his writings. Galen, a Greek physician and author, wrote about bee treatments, and Austrian physician Philip Terc wrote a paper titled "Report About a Peculiar Connection Between the Bee Stings and Rheumatism," based on clinical studies for bee stings in 1888. All of these studies spread throughout Europe and into the United States. It was considered a "folk remedy," but professionals in the medical field began to investigate its usage on a pharmacological level. Doctors started using the venom in injections for therapy. In recent times, people have begun practicing this kind of therapy by themselves without the help of professionals.

Bee venom is a viable commodity and used by people all over the world. Russia is best known today for using bee venom in therapy, but it is becoming more common across the globe. The clear, watery liquid is odorless. It is made up of several unstable components that can be lost if not collected properly. Venom is mostly water, with the remainder being a certain amount of proteins, peptides, sugars, and acids, many of which are also contained in a bee's blood. Melittin is the main chemical compound found in bee venom. It is a very potent anti-inflammation agent. The other compounds provide pain relief and alter nerve pathway transmissions.

Venom is sought after mostly for the physiological effects it has on the human body. Traditional medicine has used bee venom for centuries in the treatment of rheumatism.

Bee venom therapy, or apitherapy, has been used to treat a long list of ailments like arthritis, epilepsy, asthma, myositis, neuralgia, malaria, and even temporary relief of cancer. It has been found that beekeepers who are often stung rarely have problems with their joints or muscles. Recently, bee venom has been deliberately used in the treatment of neurological disorders, such as multiple-sclerosis.

Bee venom can be used through natural bee stings, subcutaneous injections, electrophoresis, ointments, inhalations, or tablets, but it is a very dangerous substance. Bee venom therapy should only be performed by someone with extensive knowledge.

The venom is obtained by some doctors in glass vials to be injected under their patient's skin. There are few side effects, but the idea is to actually create some inflammation, swelling, and itching. A few manufacturers provide high-quality venom products in the form of a balm or cream to be applied directly to the infected area. Many patients prefer this method.

Bee venom can be sold in any form, including whole bee extract, pure liquid venom, an injectable solution, and — most often — as dry crystals. It is complete in any form and ready for sale. Preparing the venom for sale must be done in extremely clean and hygienic conditions, considering it will be used on humans.

Bee venom extraction kits and myriad containers for storage and sale are available throughout the Internet. There are also tutorials and training courses online and in many communities.

Propolis

Propolis is the "bee glue" that bees make from the substances they gather from plants and trees. It is what they use to do various tasks in the hive like cover holes and make repairs. Bees use propolis because of its amazing antimicrobial properties to sterilize their home and make repairs.

It is necessary to remove it all from the top edges of your supers, or it will be difficult to open the hive during the winter. Propolis is extremely sticky when it is warm and when it is cooled; it becomes a glue that is nearly impossible to break through.

The best way to remove propolis is with a trap. Propolis traps are similar to queen extruders because they are constructed of a screen that is laid across the top bars of the hive. The trap must be small enough so that bees cannot squeeze through it. If the bees cannot get through the space, they will instinctively fill the holes with propolis. When it is full, you can remove and store it. When you are ready to use it, chill for a few hours, then smack it hard against an object; it will shatter into pieces that you can pick up and work with.

Propolis has several uses, from a tincture similar to iodine to a cream for scrapes, cuts, and minor abrasions.

To make a tincture, place one cup each of propolis and pure grain alcohol in a pot with a tight-fitting lid; heat on low. Every 10 to 15 minutes, shake the pan gently without removing the lid. Once is the mixture has completely dissolved, allow it to cool and strain through a coffee filter; place in a bottle when cool.

To make a cream, melt one tablespoon each of beeswax, propolis, honey, and paraffin. Once the mixture is cooled, pour into jars.

Mead

One of the most well-known honey products is mead. It is known as the drink of the gods, as Zeus was said to have consumed it regularly. The ancient Druids also produced and consumed mead. During the Middle Ages, it was wildly popular in the northernmost regions of Europe, where wine grapes were not easy to grow. With its past in the hands of the great gods, as well as in the tales of Druids and Viking warriors with great goblets of the golden liquid, most people who have never tried mead are in for quite a surprise upon their first sip. It is an amazingly delicious and delicate drink.

Mead is an alcoholic drink made from honey, water, and yeast that has been allowed to ferment. In the simplest of terms, it is a wine made from honey instead of grapes. It can also be made with a variety of fruits and spices. Mead is sometimes called by other names, depending on what fruits and spices have been used in its production. It is most often a clear liquid that has a slight golden tint. The alcohol level ranges between 7 percent and 24 percent, and it can have a dry or very full taste. The taste (dry or sweet) depends on when the fermentation was stopped and the amounts of honey and water used in proportion to each other. It can taste as light as a white grape juice, and as rich and full as a dessert wine. If the fermenting process continues while the product is bottled, it results in a bubbly drink similar to champagne. There are various types of mead and recipes, each with its own specific name:

- Basic mead is made of honey and water.

- Sack mead is very strong mead made with extra honey.

- Braggot is mead made of honey and malt.

- Capisicumel is mead made from honey and chile pepper.

- Cyser mead is made from honey and apples.

- Hippocras is mead made from honey, grapes, and spices.

Mead is brewed and then allowed to ferment. The yeast is the worker bee in this instance and does all the work of turning the mixture into a delicious beverage. Many beekeepers who have experience in this honey product suggest that boiling should be avoided; the mixture should be brought to a temperature just below boiling to allow the best flavor of the honey to shine through in the finished product.

The biggest downside to making your own mead is that it takes a long time. Six months is the average time most beekeepers will allow their mead to ferment. It can be longer, but certainly not shorter.

One important part of mead making is cleanliness. It is imperative to keep everything clean and sanitary. Using a bleach soak is one technique. Soak everything in a bucket of bleach for several hours before beginning. The yeast involved with the capped jug is like an incubator. As the yeast begins to work, it can become a hotbed for many types of bacteria to grow. Keeping the entire workplace sterile, as well as the utensils and equipment, is essential to making great mead.

For those who plan to sell their mead, a few tools are needed, such as a fermenter, a glass carboy, and an airlock. If you plan to sell your product, those items are necessary. For mead makers who simply want to experiment, you will need a few basic supplies: a gallon jug of spring water, a packet of yeast, a balloon, a rubber band, 2 to 3 pounds of honey, a small box of raisins, a sliced apple, and a clove.

Begin the process by pouring half of the water into a clean, sterile container. Place the honey in a sink full of warm water to make it easier to pour. Place the apple, the honey, half the box of raisins, a small clove, and the package of yeast into the jug. Add enough water until the level reaches 3 to 4 inches below the top of the jug. Cap the jug and shake vigorously for at least five minutes. The shaking mixes the yeast and also adds air to the mixture. The yeast needs a lot of air for the mead to taste its very best.

Remove the cap and put the balloon over the mouth of the jug. Wrap a rubber band around the mouth of the balloon to keep it in place. If the balloon seems to be getting too big, poke a hole in it; it will allow some of the gases to escape while keeping it protected from impurities.

Once the balloon starts to inflate, the process of mead making is under way. The gases that are forming inside the jug are gathering in the balloon. Set the jug inside a cabinet that stays cool and dark. Check it frequently to make sure the balloon is still in place.

By the third week, the balloon will deflate, signaling that fermentation is complete. Pour the liquid into a strainer then into another clean glass jug. Strain all the fruit and spices from the mixture into the new jug and put a clean balloon over the mouth of that jug.

Place the new jug into a cool, dry storage space. Leave for five months. Check on it every few days and watch as it grows clearer. Mead can also be entered in competitions and sold at novelty events like Renaissance fairs and Medieval festivals.

You can package and label your mead if you intend to sell it or give it as gifts. If you have chosen a name for your mead, make sure it is prominently displayed on the label. This enables your brand of this unique beverage to gather a foothold in the business.

Include information such as all ingredients used and the date it began to ferment next to the date it was bottled and packaged. True mead drinkers enjoy having this information and are hesitant to purchase or drink anything without this information. Remember once again: If you sell any food or beverage from your home, you must have a license.

Chapter 8

Cooking With Honey

There are a few details you should keep in mind when cooking with honey. Honey is sticky and can be a mess to clean up. If you coat your measuring utensils with a quick blast of nonstick spray, then the honey slides right off, and the utensil can be easily cleaned.

Honey is a great sweetener and, because it contains no fat, it is a good substitute for sugar. It also gives baked goods a gorgeous golden color and keeps them moist and fresh longer. While this is a delicious alternative to sugar, there are a few factors to remember:

- Honey is higher in fructose and sweeter than sugar, so use less honey in any recipe when substituting for sugar.

- To modify your favorite recipes with honey, start by replacing half of the sugar. If that works well, try replacing all of the sugar.

- Lessen the amount of liquids used in the recipe by ¼ cup for every cup of honey.

- Add ½ teaspoon of baking soda for every cup of honey in the recipe.

- Lower the temperature of the oven by about 25° to avoid excessive browning.

Author's Apiary

Using bee products for your cooking

Cooking with honey can be tricky. It makes foods sweeter than sugar and can be used as a thickening agent. If honey is being used as a substitute for sugar, reduce the amount of honey by ¼, ⅓, or ½. It is also a good idea to reduce the oven temperature by about 25° to 30°.

Honey is known to turn cakes, pies, cookies, breads, and other baked goods a golden brown, but use caution, because honey can brown quickly. Use a pinch of baking soda to counter that effect.

It is best to clean up spills while the honey is warm or to use a hot, soapy towel. It also helps to coat all forks, spoons, and other cooking utensils and surfaces with a nonstick cooking spray.

Recipes

Recipes reprinted with permission from the National Honey Board. The National Honey Board does not support any unsubstantiated claims ascribed to honey.

Beverages

Honey Lemonade

Yield: 8 servings

Ingredients:

1 cup honey
2 cups lemon juice
10 cups water

Instructions:

Combine lemon juice and honey in a large carafe, stirring constantly until honey is completely dissolved. Add water and chill.

For an additional treat, pour some of the lemonade into ice cube trays and freeze. When frozen, add to your glass of lemonade to prevent watered-down lemonade.

Strawberry-Honey Shake

Yield: 4 servings

Ingredients:

1 ½ cups 2% reduced-fat milk
15-20 strawberries with tops removed
¼ cup honey
5-10 ice cubes
1 cup plain yogurt
1 tsp vanilla extract

Instructions:

Mix all ingredients together in a blender on high speed, adding ice cubes slowly until mixture is smooth and creamy. Pour into tall frozen mugs and garnish with fresh strawberries.

Spiced Tea

Yield: 6 servings

Ingredients:

6 cups brewed tea

6 cloves

½ cup honey

6 lemon wedges

6 cinnamon sticks

6 orange slices

Instructions:

Combine the tea, honey, cloves, cinnamon, and lemon in a saucepan. Simmer on low heat for five to ten minutes. Strain and serve warm with a garnish of orange slices, or serve over ice. Add a sprig of mint for a boost of flavor.

*Frosty Honey Latte

Yield: 4 servings

Ingredients:

2 cups double-strength brewed coffee

1 cup 2% reduced-fat milk

¼ cup honey

2 cups ice

Instructions:

Whisk coffee, milk, and honey in large pitcher until honey dissolves. Chill and blend coffee mixture with ice in blender until frothy before serving.

*Golden Honey Margarita

Yield: 1 beverage

Ingredients:

1 oz. gold tequila
½ oz triple sec
1 oz Honey Simple Syrup (honey and warm water mixed in equal parts)
2 ½ oz margarita mix

Combine ingredients and use shaker to shake with ice. Pour into cocktail glass that has been garnished with salt and lime.

*Agua de Sandia (Watermelon)

Yield: 2 quarts

Ingredients:

1 medium watermelon (peeled, seeded, and chopped)
1 to 1 ½ cups honey
2 quarts water
2 limes, thinly sliced (optional)

Instructions:

Puree chopped watermelon, 1 cup water, and 1 cup honey until smooth. Pour puree into a pitcher. Mix in the rest of the water. Garnish with lime and sweeten to taste: Add additional ½ cup of honey, if needed.

*Honey Breakfast Drink

Yield: 4 servings

Ingredients:

2 cups 2% reduced-fat milk
½ cup orange juice
¼ to ½ cup honey
¼ cup low-fat dry milk
¼ cup wheat germ
1 large banana, peeled and sliced
4 to 5 ice cubes

Instructions:

Mix all ingredients in a blender.

*Pink Honey Bee

Yield: 1 beverage

Ingredients:

1 ½ oz vodka (can substitute spiced rum or citrus vodka)
1 oz Honey Simple Syrup (honey and warm water mixed in equal parts)
2 oz sweet & sour sauce
1 oz cranberry juice

Instructions:

Pour ingredients in shaker, shake with ice. Strain into cocktail glass that has been garnished with a cherry.

Baked Goods

*Bee Sweet Banana Bread

Yield: 1 loaf

Ingredients:

½ cup honey

⅓ cup butter or margarine

1 tsp vanilla

2 eggs

½ cup all-purpose flour

¾ cup whole-wheat flour

½ cup quick-cooking oats

1 tsp baking powder

½ tsp salt

1 tsp ground nutmeg

1 cup mashed ripe banana

½ cup chopped walnuts

Instructions:

Use an electric mixer to cream the honey and butter in a large bowl, then add in vanilla. Add eggs, one at a time, and beat the mixture after each egg is added. Combine both flours, with the oats, baking powder, salt, and nutmeg in a small bowl. Add the honey mixture and bananas before stirring in the walnuts. Place batter in a greased and floured 9 x 5 x 3-inch loaf pan. Bake at 325°F for 50 minutes. Cool in pan on a wire rack 15 minutes, then remove loaf from pan to cool completely.

*Apricot-Honey Bread

Yield: 12 servings

Ingredients:

3 cups whole-wheat flour

3 tsp baking powder

1 tsp ground cinnamon

½ tsp salt

¼ tsp ground nutmeg

1 ¼ cups 2% reduced-fat milk

1 cup honey

1 egg, slightly beaten

2 Tbs vegetable oil

1 cup chopped dried apricots

½ cup sunflower seeds, chopped walnuts, or chopped almonds

½ cup raisins

Instructions:

Combine flour, baking power, cinnamon, salt, and nutmeg in large bowl. Then combine milk, honey, egg, and oil in a different bowl. Pour the liquid mixture over dry ingredients and stir until it becomes moist. Gently fold in apricots, sunflower seeds, and raisins. Pour into greased 9 x 5 x 3-inch loaf pan. Bake at 350°F for one hour.

*Easy Honey Muffins

Yield: 12 muffins

Ingredients:

½ cup 2% reduced-fat milk

¼ cup honey

1 egg, beaten

2 ½ cups buttermilk baking mix

Instructions:

Mix milk, honey, and egg. Add baking mix and stir until moist. Place mixture into greased muffin pans. Bake at 400°F for 20 minutes.

*Holiday Honey Cookies

Yield: 4 dozen gingerbread men

Ingredients:

7 ½ cups all-purpose flour

1 Tbs baking soda

2 Tbs cinnamon

1 Tbs ginger

1 tsp nutmeg

½ tsp salt

1 ½ cups (3 sticks) butter

1 ½ cups dark brown sugar

1 tsp lemon zest

¾ cup honey

3 eggs

Instructions:

Sift flour, baking soda, cinnamon, ginger, nutmeg, and salt. In a separate mixing bowl, cream the butter, brown sugar, and zest. Add honey and mix until smooth. Add eggs, one at a time, and dry ingredients; mix. Divide dough into two parts, flatten, and wrap in wax paper. Refrigerate until dough is firm enough to roll, about 30 minutes. Roll dough to ¼-inch thickness and cut with cookie cutters. Bake at 350°F oven for 15 minutes.

*Dates and Honey Bread

Yield: 1 loaf

Ingredients:

2 ½ cups all-purpose flour

2 tsp baking powder

1 tsp baking soda

¾ tsp salt

1 tsp ground cinnamon

1 tsp ground nutmeg

¼ tsp ground allspice

¼ tsp ground ginger

¾ cup pitted and chopped dates or raisins

½ cup pecans, chopped

¾ cup buttermilk

¾ cup honey

2 Tbs molasses

1 egg

Instructions:

Mix the flour, baking powder, baking soda, salt, and spices in a large bowl. Add dates and nuts; set aside. Beat the buttermilk, honey, oil, molasses, and egg, and add mixture to the dry ingredients. Grease a 9 x 5 x 3-inch loaf pan and pour in the batter. Bake at 325°F for one hour and cool.

*Honey and Lemon Green Tea Cupcakes

Yield: 12-14 cupcakes

Ingredients:

1 green tea bag
½ cup boiling water
2 cups unbleached all-purpose flour
½ tsp baking soda
½ tsp baking powder
½ tsp salt
Zest and juice (¼ cup) of one lemon
¼ cup buttermilk
½ cup butter, softened
¾ cup Orange Blossom honey
2 large eggs

Instructions:

Pour boiling water over tea bag and let sit for 3 minutes, then cool tea. Sift flour, baking soda, baking powder, and salt. Combine green tea, lemon zest and juice, and buttermilk. Cream butter in mixing bowl and add honey and eggs. Add half of the dry mixture to the creamed ingredients and mix on low. Slowly add the tea mixture and add the rest of the dry ingredients until just combined. Line muffin tins with paper and fill muffin tins ⅔ full. Bake 18 minutes. Remove to wire rack; cool. Frost and decorate if desired.

Honey-Nut Roll

Yield: 16 servings

Ingredients:

1 box hot roll mix
3 Tbs honey
1 stick butter (softened)
¼ cup cinnamon
2 cups walnuts
½ cup sugar

Instructions:

Follow the directions on the box for preparing the hot roll mix. Roll dough out into a large rectangle shape. Spread butter evenly over entire sheet of dough. Drizzle two tablespoons of the honey over the butter. Sprinkle on walnuts, cinnamon, and sugar. Roll the entire mixture into a long tube. Curve into a horseshoe shape and bake according to package directions. Remove from oven and let cool slightly, then drizzle with remaining tablespoon of honey. Cut into ½-inch slices and serve warm.

Honey Spice Cake

Yield: 12 servings

Ingredients:

3 eggs

2 cups flour

1 cup oil

2 tsp baking soda

1 cup honey

1 tsp salt

1 cup buttermilk

1 tsp nutmeg, cinnamon, or allspice

1 cup applesauce

Instructions:

Beat eggs, oil, honey, buttermilk, and applesauce until smooth, then add the remaining dry ingredients. Stir well. Pour batter into a greased and lightly floured 9 x 13 pan. Bake at 350°F for 35 to 40 minutes.

Sauces and Marinades

Honey BBQ Sauce
(courtesy of Houston "Lucky" Burgess)

Ingredients:

1 cup honey

1 tsp black pepper

2 cups ketchup

1 tsp garlic

1 Tbs red pepper

1 tsp parsley flakes

2 tsp vinegar

Instructions:

Stir all ingredients together until fully mixed. Let ingredients sit overnight in the refrigerator.

Italian Honey Marinade

Ingredients:

1 cup olive oil

1 Tbs garlic

¼ cup red wine vinegar

1 Tbs fresh lemon zest

¼ cup honey

1 Tbs basil

1 Tbs rosemary

1 Tbs parsley

Instructions:

Mix all ingredients well. Cover and let it sit 12 to 24 hours, shaking occasionally.

*Vegetables with Spicy Honey Peanut Sauce

Yield: 6 servings

Ingredients:

½ cup honey

¼ cup peanut butter

2 Tbs soy sauce

1 Tbs chopped fresh cilantro

⅛ tsp crushed red pepper flakes

4 cups broccoli florets

4 cups sliced carrots

4 cups snow peas

6 cups cooked white rice

Instructions:

Mix honey, peanut butter, soy sauce, cilantro, and red pepper flakes. Steam vegetables and toss with peanut sauce before serving.

*Arugula Salad with Honey-Herb Dressing

Yield: 4 servings

Ingredients:

4 cups arugula leaves

1 cup cherry tomatoes

1 cup mushrooms, sliced

1 cup Parmesan cheese, sliced croutons, or toasted bread slices

¼ cup lemon juice

2 Tbs honey

2 Tbs olive oil

½ tsp dried basil

½ tsp dried coriander

Salt, to taste

Instructions:

Combine arugula leaves, cherry tomatoes, and mush-rooms. Cover and refrigerate. Mix lemon juice, honey, olive oil, dried basil, dried coriander, and salt in a jar, close lid tightly, and shake until mixed. Top salad with Parmesan and dressing; toss.

*Herb Garden Dip or Dressing

Yield: 20 servings

Ingredients:

1 pint sour cream
6 Tbs honey
2 Tbs orange juice, thawed, undiluted
2 Tbs Dijon mustard
2 tsp cream-style horseradish
2 tsp rosemary, crushed
1 tsp chervil, crushed
1 tsp basil, crushed
¾ tsp salt
½ tsp white pepper
¼ tsp garlic powder

Instructions:

Mix all ingredients. Cover and refrigerate for a few hours. Stir before using.

Side Dishes

Honey Mashed Potatoes

Yield: 4 to 6 servings

Ingredients:

6 – 8 russet potatoes
1 tsp salt
2 Tbs honey
1 tsp black pepper
¼ cup milk

Instructions:

Peel and pare the potatoes. Boil in a pot of slightly salted water until tender. Drain potatoes and place in a mixing bowl. Add honey, salt, pepper, and milk. Use an electric or hand mixer to whip potatoes until creamy. Add extra milk for creamier potatoes.

Honey Carrots

Yield: 4 to 6 servings

Ingredients:

1 lb fresh carrots
1 tsp salt
½ cup honey
1 tsp black pepper

Instructions:

Peel and chop ends off carrots. Cut into bite-size pieces or medallions. Boil in a pot of slightly salted water until tender. Drain water and add the honey, salt, and black pepper to the carrots. Stir until cooked. Serve warm.

Honey Sweet Potatoes

Yield: 2 servings

Ingredients:

3 large sweet potatoes
2 Tbs cooking oil
½ cup honey
Salt (optional)

Instructions:

Wash and slice the sweet potatoes in approximately quarter-inch slices. Lay slices of sweet potatoes in a single layer on a plate or baking sheet. Cover both sides with honey. Use a basting brush if necessary.

Once the slices of sweet potato are completely covered, place in a skillet of hot oil. Fry for one minute and flip. Both sides should be light brown. Remove from heat and place on a paper towel to soak up excess oil; salt lightly.

*Balsamic Onions with Honey

Yield: 6 servings

Ingredients:

3 large red onions (about 3 lbs)
1 Tbs and ¼ cup water
6 Tbs honey
¼ cup balsamic vinegar or red-wine vinegar
3 Tbs butter or margarine, melted
1 tsp paprika
1 tsp ground coriander
½ tsp salt
⅛ tsp ground red pepper

Instructions:

Cut peeled onions into halves. Place onion halves cut-side down in greased baking dish. Sprinkle with 1 tablespoon of water and cover with foil. Bake at 350°F for 30 minutes. Then mix honey, vinegar, the remaining ¼ cup water, butter, paprika, coriander, salt, and red pepper in small bowl. Remove onions from oven and turn them so the cut side is facing up. Cover honey mixture over onions and bake, uncovered, for 15 more minutes.

*Honey-Dill Coleslaw

Yield: 4 servings

Ingredients:

¼ cup honey

½ cup sour cream

½ tsp dried dill weed

16 oz coleslaw mix

¼ cup thinly sliced onion

Salt and pepper, to taste

Instructions:

Combine honey, sour cream, and dill. In a different bowl, toss coleslaw mix with honey-dill mixture. Season to taste.

*Honey Cream Cheese Tea Sandwiches

Yield: 7 servings

Ingredients:

Any variety bread slices

3 oz cream cheese, softened

2 Tbs honey

½ tsp grated orange peel

Watercress sprigs

Orange peel (with white part of peel removed)

Instructions:

Cut bread into desired finger-sandwich shapes and remove crust, if desired. Blend cream cheese, honey, and grated orange peel. Spread mixture on bread and garnish with watercress sprigs or orange peel.

*Honey Kiwi-Raspberry Fruit Dip

Yield: about 2 cups

Ingredients:

1 ripe kiwi, peeled and diced
½ cup unsweetened frozen raspberries
½ cup pure honey
8 oz low-fat vanilla yogurt
Fresh fruit, for dipping

Instructions:

Puree kiwi, raspberries, and honey in food processor. Stir in yogurt and serve with sliced fresh fruit.

Main Dishes

Honey-Sweetened Salmon Fillets

Yield: 6 servings

Ingredients:

6 large salmon fillets
4 Tbs fresh cilantro (chopped)
3 Tbs honey
½ tsp salt
4 green onions (thinly sliced)
1 tsp canned jalapeno peppers (chopped)
½ cup red onion (thinly sliced)
½ cup frozen corn
3 Tbs white wine vinegar

2 Tbs vegetable oil

3 Tbs freshly squeezed lime juice

Instructions:

Set aside honey, corn, and salmon. Mix together the remaining ingredients. Sauté corn in heated vegetable oil until warm and add to other ingredients. Sauté salmon in the vegetable oil until fully cooked, 3 to 5 minutes per side. Trickle honey over the salmon as it cooks. Place salmon on a plate; put two tablespoons of chopped vegetable mixture on the top of each fillet.

Honey-Baked Citrus Ham

Yield: 6 to 8 servings

Ingredients:

5 – 10 lb ham

¼ cup cloves

3 cups honey

½ cup butter

½ cup orange juice

½ cup brown sugar

Instructions:

Warm the honey, orange juice, butter, and brown sugar until mixed together well. Use a meat injector to inject the ham with the mixture. Score the ham in 1-inch intervals and insert cloves. Place the ham on a foil-lined baking dish and bake according to directions.

Honey-Baked Chicken

Yield: 4 servings

Ingredients:

4 – 5 lb roaster
2 Tbs white-wine vinegar
½ cup honey
Olive oil cooking spray

Instructions:

Lightly coat the roaster with the cooking spray. Set aside in a baking dish. Mix together vinegar and honey. Pierce the chicken in several places with a fork and slowly pour the mixture over it. Bake until chicken is golden brown (approximately 1 hour, 30 minutes) in a 350°F oven.

*A Honey of a Chili

Yield: 8 servings

Ingredients:

1 package (15 oz) firm tofu
1 Tbs vegetable oil
1 cup chopped onion
¾ cup chopped green bell pepper
2 cloves garlic, finely chopped
2 Tbs chili powder
1 tsp ground cumin
1 tsp salt
½ tsp dried oregano

½ tsp crushed red pepper flakes

1 can (28 oz) diced tomatoes, undrained

1 can (15 ½ oz) red kidney beans, undrained

1 can (8 oz) tomato sauce

¼ cup honey

2 Tbs red-wine vinegar

Instructions:

Use a cheese grater to shred tofu. Freeze overnight in an airtight container. Thaw tofu in strainer to remove extra liquid. Heat oil in a saucepan until hot and stir in onion, green pepper, and garlic until tender. Stir in chili powder, cumin, salt, oregano, and crushed red pepper. Add tofu; cook for one minute. Stir in diced tomatoes, kidney beans, tomato sauce, honey, and vinegar, and boil. Reduce heat and simmer for 20 minutes.

*Asian Honey-Tea Grilled Prawns

Yield: 4 servings

Ingredients:

1 ½ lbs medium shrimp, peeled and deveined
Salt
2 green onions, thinly sliced
1 cup brewed, double-strength orange spice tea, cooled
¼ cup honey
¼ cup rice vinegar
¼ cup soy sauce
1 Tbs fresh ginger, peeled and finely chopped
½ tsp ground black pepper

Instructions:

Combine all ingredients except for the shrimp, salt, and onions to make the marinade in a plastic bag. Remove ½ cup marinade for dipping sauce. Add shrimp to marinade and securely close the bag. Turn the bag to coat the shrimp. Place bag in refrigerator for a time period between 30 minutes to 12 hours. Once marinated, take the shrimp out of the bag and place onto skewers, spacing them evenly. Grill for 4 to 6 minutes, or until shrimp are firm to the touch. Season as desired. Meanwhile, boil the dipping sauce from the extra marinade (½ cup) for 3 to 5 minutes and stir in green onions.

*Caribbean Honey-Spiced Chicken with Mango

Yield: 4 servings

Ingredients:

¼ cup honey

¼ cup fresh lemon juice

2 tsp freshly grated lemon peel

1 ripe mango, peeled and diced

1 small onion, peeled and quartered

2 fresh jalapeno peppers, halved and seeded

2 tsp paprika

2 tsp vegetable oil

1 ½ tsp garlic salt

½ tsp ground cinnamon

½ tsp freshly ground black pepper

½ tsp ground allspice

4 boneless, skinless chicken breast halves

1 Tbs vegetable oil

Instructions:

Whisk honey, lemon juice, and lemon peel in small bowl. Take out ¼ cup of the mixture and place in food processor. Add mango to the mixture that is still in the bowl and toss ingredients. Place bowl in refrigerator. Add onion, jalapenos, paprika, oil, garlic salt, cinnamon, pepper, and allspice to the ¼-cup mixture; set aside. Use food processor until ingredients are finely chopped. Spread mixture on both sides of chicken. Place in greased baking pan and bake at 375°F for 30 minutes or until cooked. Top with reserved mango.

*Honey and Almond Sauced Cornish Game Hen

Yield: 4 servings

Ingredients:

1 cup onion, chopped

4 sprigs parsley, tied with string

1 Tbs vegetable oil

2 tsp black pepper

2 tsp ground cinnamon

1 clove garlic, to taste

Saffron, to taste

Salt, to taste

Water, as needed

1 cup honey

1 cup seedless raisins

4 Rock Cornish game hens

⅔ cup almonds, sliced, toasted

2 Tbs sesame seeds, toasted

Instructions:

Sauté onions and parsley in oil. Mix in spices and use to season game hens. Bake at 375°F for 25 minutes. Take out parsley and discard. Put ½ inch water in bottom of pan, coat hens with honey, and add raisins. Change oven temperature to 350°F and bake for 15 minutes. Spoon pan sauce over hens and garnish with sliced almonds, sesame seeds, crisp greens, and fresh fruit.

Honey-Shrimp Tortellini

Yield: 4 servings

Ingredients:

1 lb medium shrimp (peeled and deveined)
1 ½ lb tortellini (cooked)
1 large red onion (diced)
½ cup honey
1 cup scallions (sliced)
Olive oil
4 large stalks of celery (chopped)
Parsley sprigs
2 cups of broccoli florets

Instructions:

Stir fry vegetables and shrimp in the olive oil over medium heat until the vegetables are tender-crisp and the shrimp turns pink.

Slowly drizzle half of the honey over the vegetables and shrimp; mix gently. Toss in the tortellini and drizzle remaining honey over the entire mixture. Gently mix. Garnish with parsley sprigs.

Honey-BBQ Beef Ribs

Yield: 4 servings

Ingredients:

5 lbs beef ribs
1 Tbs red pepper

1½ cups honey

1 tsp salt

½ cup green onions (chopped)

Instructions:

Boil ribs in pot of hot water for 30 minutes. Remove from water and place in a large bowl. Pour honey over ribs and toss until fully covered. Add green onions and stir into ribs and honey. Place ribs on grill or broiler pan. Sprinkle with salt and red pepper.

Grill until fully cooked, being careful not to scorch and burn.

Sweet Little Extras

Mix honey with butter and a touch of fruit juice and drizzle over angel food cake.

Mix an 8-oz package of cream cheese with an ⅛ cup honey to make a creamy and sweet cupcake frosting.

No-Bake Cookie
(Courtesy of Lynda Cook Rizzardi)

Yield: 46 to 48 cookies

Ingredients:

1 cup peanut butter

1 cup wheat bran

1 cup honey

1 cup powdered milk

1 cup powdered sugar
2 cups crisp rice cereal

Instructions:

Mix the peanut butter and honey together. Add each of the remaining ingredients, one at a time, and mix well. Roll into small balls and refrigerate for several hours. Sprinkle with powdered sugar and enjoy.

Alternatively: Melt one pound of white chocolate almond bark in a double boiler with a tablespoon of shortening. Dip the balls into the chocolate mixture, then place on a waxed-paper-lined tray. Chill for a few minutes in the refrigerator to set the coating. Place in an airtight container. *Delicious!*

*Paraguay Honey and Peanut Candy

Yield: 8-10 servings

Ingredients:

2 cups pure honey
1 lb toasted whole peanuts
8-10 small paper candy cups

Instructions:

Boil honey over high heat, then lower to medium heat and stir until you can see the pot's bottom. Add peanuts and continue to stir over medium heat for 3 to 4 minutes. Pour

1-2 Tbs of mixture into the paper candy cups and freeze for 15 minutes.

Resources

Online Resources for Beekeeping Fun:

http://maarec.cas.psu.edu/pdfs/beeswax.pdf
www.apis.me
www.apiservices.com
www.badbeekeeping.com
www.bee-commerce.com
www.beehoo.com
www.beevenom.com
www.mybeehives.com

Other Resources:

A.I. Root Company 623 W. Liberty St., Medina, OH 44256
Alberta Honey Producers Co-op, Box 3909, Spruce Grove, Alberta, T7X 3B1
Dadant and Sons, 51 S. 2nd Street, Hamilton, IL 62341
Mann Lake Bee Supplies, 1-800-880-7694 (in Minnesota)
Western Bee Supply, P.O. Box 171, Polson, MT 59860
Walter T. Kelley Company, P.O. Box 240, Clarkson, KY 42726

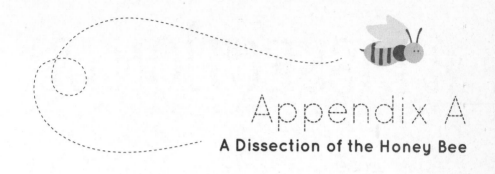

Appendix A

A Dissection of the Honey Bee

The wings and stingers characterize a honey bee, along with its yellow and black stripes, but what other body parts does it have? With three body segments, the honey bee is a complex creature. Use this appendix to learn about the parts of the bee and where each part is located on the body.

a DISSECTION OF

A. Antennae

B. Head

C. Compound eye

D. Simple eye

E. Tube-like tongue (proboscis)

F. Mandibles (jaws)

G. Thorax

H. Six-jointed legs

I. Pollen basket

J. Hindwing

K. Forewing

L. Abdomen

M. Wax glands under the abdomen

N. Stinger (only in females)

O. Black stripes on abdomen

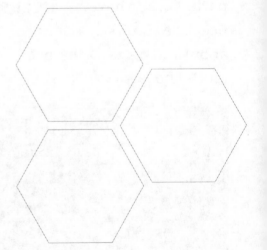

THE HONEY BEE

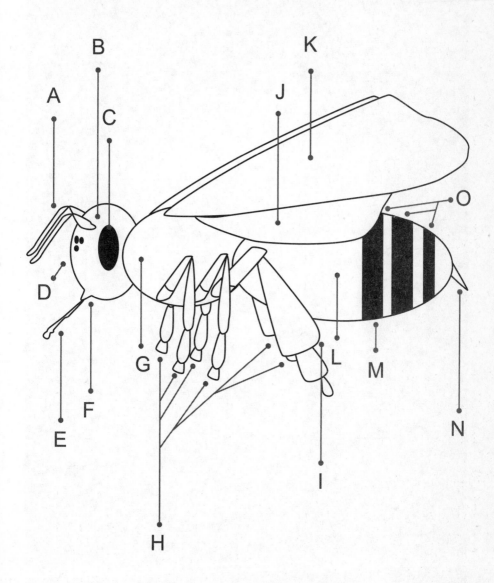

Appendix B

How Bees Work: The Life Cycle

Like butterflies and other insects, bees go through many stages of life. Starting as an egg, the bee grows over time until it is big enough to leave the hive. From that point on, the life span of the bee varies depending on the bee's role: A queen bee can live for two years, drones die immediately after mating with queens, and worker bees can live from 40 days to 140 days, depending on the season. Use this Appendix to learn about the honey bee's life cycle before leaving the hive.

HOW BEES WORK:

Queen bee lays egg in a wax shell → Worker bees feed the hatched larva → Larva reaches full growth

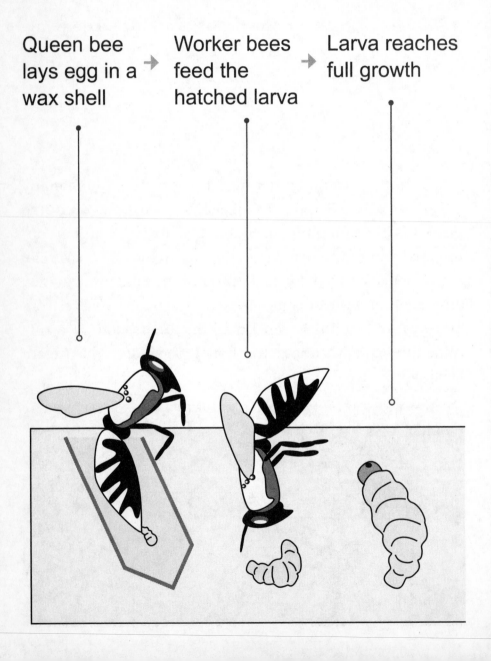

THE LiFE CYCLE

Workers seal cell with wax → Larva spins cocoon and changes into pupa → Adult bee leaves cell

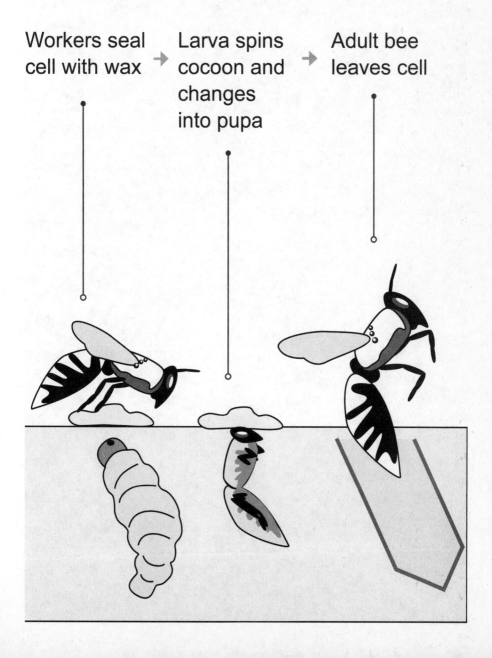

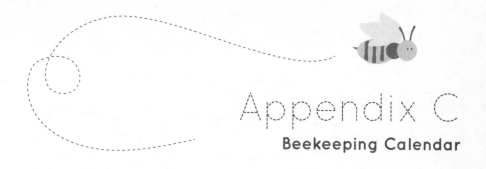

To keep track of hive activity, here is a list of activities taking place each month. There are also suggestions of activities the beekeeper should perform, along with an approximate timeframe to be spent with your bees each month.

january

The bees. Thousands of workers huddle around the queen bee amidst their winter cluster. Little activity occurs, with the exception of cleansing flights on warm days (around 50°F.) In the absence of drones, a few worker broods will appear in the hive. The bees will take in around 25 pounds of honey during this month.

The beekeeper. Minimal work from you will be necessary at the hives. When heavy snow accumulates, be sure to clear the hive entrance in order to provide ventilation. Use this month to conduct further research on bees, partake in bee club meetings, and prepare next season's equipment. Be sure to contact a credible supplier and order packaged bees, if necessary.

Time spent: Less than an hour.

Provided by Amy Grisak

february

The bees. While comfy in the cluster, the queen bee will start laying a few more eggs per day. Though only females are permitted in the hive, worker bees will start taking cleansing flights on warmer days. Again, the bees consume 25 pounds of honey this month.

The beekeeper. Like January, there is not much for you to do aside from attending bee club meetings and reading up on your bees. It is wise to prepare your spring equipment, too.

Time spent: Less than an hour.

march

The bees. During this month, there is a risk of colonies dying off due to starvation. This can be prevented by giving the bees a lot of sugar syrup during the fall. As the length of days increases, the queen gradually increases the number of eggs she lays. With more brood, the drones start to show up, and a larger amount of food is taken in by the bees. Honey stores are still consumed by the bees.

The beekeeper. On a nice, warm day, take a glance into the hive. Without removing the frames, glance under the cover. Emergency feeding may be required if no sealed honey appears in the top frames. Continue the feeding until the bees are gathering their own food supplies. At this time, be sure to add Apistan® strips (leave in the hive for 45 days).

> **Time spent: 2 hours.**

Provided by Amy Grisak

april

The bees. As the weather improves, early blossoms start to surface. As bees are bringing pollen in, the queen is occupied in the hive laying eggs, causing the population to grow rapidly. The drones start to show up, as well.

The beekeeper. Conduct a thorough inspection on the first warm, calm day. Can you spot the queen along with eggs and brood? Is there a nice egg-laying pattern? During the later period of the month, you may want to reverse the hive deeps. The broods will be adequately distributed, and the growth of the colony will be positively impacted. Start feeding the hive with a mix of medicated syrup and menthol, which serves as mite control.

Time spent: 3 hours.

Provided by the USDA

may

The bees. Activity increases this month as nectar and pollen is coming into the hive thickly and quickly. With the queen's achieving her highest rate of egg laying, the hive will be bustling with activity.

The beekeeper. Apistan strips may be removed, if they have been present in the hive for 45 days. Menthol also needs to be taken away. Add on a queen excluder, putting honey supers at the top of the top deep. Beware of swarming, and examine the hive on a weekly basis. Continue to partake in bee club meetings and workshops.

Time spent: 4-5 hours.

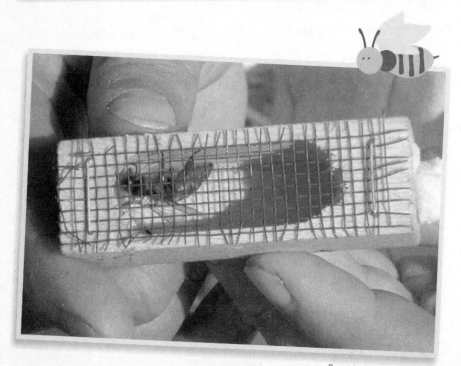

Provided by Amy Grisak

june

The bees. Although the queen's rate of laying eggs may decrease a bit this month, the unswarmed colonies will be filled with bees. The primary flow of honey will occur.

The beekeeper. Examine the hive on a weekly basis to ensure that it is healthy and that the queen is there. Continue to add on honey supers and inspect swarms. Again, participate in bee club meetings and workshops.

Time spent: 4-5 hours.

Provided by FDACS-DPI (University of Florida)

july

The bees. Weather permitting, the flow of nectar may continue. On hot nights, bees may be seen trying to cool off on the hive's exterior.

The beekeeper. Ensure the health of your colony by adding additional honey supers, if needed, and conducting regular inspections.

Time spent: 2-3 hours.

august

The bees. With the decrease in nectar flow, the growth of the colony is deterred. Nevertheless, drones are still around the hive.

The beekeeper. Relax, because there is not much for you to do this month. There is no chance for swarming. Keep an eye out for honey robbing by other bees.

> **Time spent: About 1-2 hours.**

september

The bees. This month, a decrease in hive population and the queen's egg laying is evident. Drones may start to vanish.

The beekeeper. While harvesting the honey crop, do not forget to allot 60 pounds of honey for the colony to use during the winter. Be sure the queen is present, and feed and medicate once the end of the month is near (only medicate the first 2 gallons). Apistan strips need to be added and remain in the hive for 42 days. Additionally, menthol should be applied for mite control. Do not stop feeding the bees until they will take in no more syrup. Participate in bee club meetings.

Time spent: 2-3 hours.

october

The bees. Preparing for the winter, the bees do not show much activity.

The beekeeper. Beware of robbing. To provide ventilation for the bees, put inner cover wedges in the hive. Place a mouse guard at the hive's entrance. To ensure the colony remains dry, install Insulite® boards underneath the cover of the hive. A wind break may be constructed if needed. As you complete winter feeding, be sure to discard the Apistan strips. Again, take part in bee club meetings.

Time spent: 2 hours.

november

The bees. Activity decreases even more this month. The cold weather has the hive huddling up.

The beekeeper. Put your equipment away during the winter. Attend bee club meetings.

Time spent: About an hour.

december

The bees. The bees are tightly compacted together.

The beekeeper. Enjoy your time off, because there is nothing to do with the bees this month. Curl up with a good book about beekeeping, or attend a beekeeping club meeting.

Time spent: None.

Provided by Amy Grisak

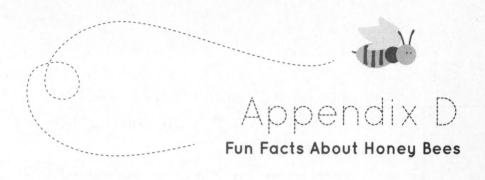

DID YOU KNOW?

Honey bees are originally from Europe. The bee species was brought to North America by early settlers.

By nature, honey bees are not aggressive, meaning that they will only sting when provoked or threatened. Stinging is usually a defense mechanism for protecting the hive.

Various bees play specific roles — the honey bees are a highly organized and structured society.

The honey bee hive is usually dormant in the winter. To stay warm, and because they are not working, honey bees survive harsh winter temperatures by forming clusters for warmth.

During the winter, honey bees self-regulate the hive's temperature, maintaining 93° Fahrenheit in the center of their bee cluster.

In one collection trip, a worker bee visits up to 100 flowers.

Depiction of bees and honey in cave paintings show that the practice of collecting honey and beekeeping has been around since ancient times.

The queen bee has the longest lifespan, living for several years. Worker bees, however, live for 6 weeks during summer, or 4-9 months during the winter.

In a lifetime, a worker bee will produce $\frac{1}{12}$ a teaspoon of honey.

Worker bees fly in hives for 55,000 miles and tap 2 million flowers just to make one pound of honey.

During honey collection, worker bees carry more than half their weight in pollen and nectar.

During the winter months, bees must produce 35 pounds of honey to have enough energy for the colony to survive.

A hive of bees can make and store up to 2 pounds of honey each day.

Each year, the average American consumes a little more than 1 pound of honey.

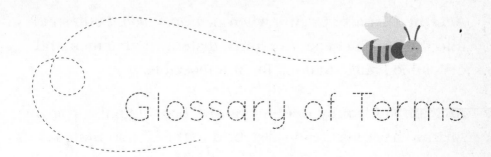

Glossary of Terms

A

Abscond: When a bee leaves the hive suddenly and without warning. This will only happen if there are terrible, intolerable problems in the hive. "The bees have absconded."

Absconding Swarm: When the whole swarm leaves the hive in search of a new place to live. This occurs when disease or hive damage becomes unmanageable.

Abdomen: A bee's third body region that houses its internal organs, including the stomachs, glands, intestine, reproductive organs, and stinger.

Abdominal Bands: The bands of extremely dense, coarse hairs around the abdomen.

Acarine Disease: Occurs when *Acarapis woodi* mites get into the bee tracheae, causing a distended abdomen and disjointed wings, making flight impossible.

Africanized Honey Bee: Aggressive bee originally from Africa. They migrated as a hybrid to the United States from South America. They are extremely ill-tempered and not suitable for keeping.

Afterswarm: When a smaller swarm leaves the hive after the larger, initial swarm; most often headed by a virgin queen. Not a common occurrence.

Alarm Pheromone: The scent that bees emit to communicate danger to each other.

Allergy: A very serious physical reaction to bee stings and bee venom. An allergy to the bees can also develop.

American Foulbrood: A serious, highly contagious bacterial disease that affects bee broods.

Anther: The male reproductive cells of a flower that produces pollen.

Antibiotics: A substance or substances that can inhibit the growth of harmful bacteria.

Apiary: Sometimes called a bee yard; it is a specific location with one or more bee hives.

Apiculture: Formal term for the science of beekeeping.

Apiculturist: A person who practices apiculture.

Apimondia: The International Federation of Beekeepers' Associations.

Apis mellifera: Scientific name of the European and Western honey bee.

Apis mellifera Carnica: Scientific name for the Carniolan bees; subspecies of the Western honey bee.

Apis mellifera Scutellata: Scientific name for the African honey bee.

Apitherapy: The practice of using honey, wax, and other bee by-products for therapeutic and medical purposes.

Automatic Uncapper: A device, typically a heated knife, that removes the wax caps from the honeycomb.

B

Bacillus thuringiensis: A natural bacteria found in soil.

Bait Hive: A bee box with a frame of honeycomb and an entrance hole used to lure swarming bees.

Balling the Queen: When workers kill an unknown, new, or aging queen by surrounding her in a tightly knit ball until she dies from overheating.

Bee Bread: A food stuff bees create; made of a mix of pollen and honey.

Bee Brush: A brush used to move bees off the comb when going through the bees.

Bee Candy: A three-to-one mixture of honey and powdered sugar. It can also be purchased as a commercial product without honey.

Bee Candy Plug: The plug used to replace the plug in a new queen's cage. It is made of bee candy and is about the size of a small bird egg.

Bee Culture: A magazine on beekeeping published by the A.I. Root Company.

Bee Escape: A piece of equipment used to make sure bees can exit the hive without re-entering.

Bee Glue: Propolis is often called bee glue because of its propensity to stick to anything.

Bee House: A small house that is just large enough for the hive and the beekeeper; used for protective purposes.

Bee Language: The movements bees make to convey information to other bees in the colony. Discovered by Karl Ritter von Frisch, who won a Nobel Prize in physiology and medicine in 1973 for his research in communication among insects.

Bee Pasture: Fields of plants, bushes, and flowering trees — wild and cultivated — that supply bees with pollen, honeydew, or nectar.

Bee Metamorphosis: The three stages of metamorphosis that a bee goes through to become a fully formed adult bee.

Beehive: The home for a colony of bees; it can be man-made or any natural structure the bees have made their home in, such as a hollow tree or crevice in a rock wall.

Bee Space: The space required between the hive parts, usually approximately ⅜-inch wide. If the space is any larger, the bees will build comb in it; any smaller, and they will fill it with propolis.

Beeswax: Secreted substance from the worker bees, used to build their comb; can be harvested and used for various purposes.

Bee Veil: Veil made from netting or fabric used to protect beekeepers from stings.

Bee Venom: Poison secreted from a bee's stinger.

Bee Year: A bee's year begins in August because the bees hatched at this time will take care of the spring population.

Begging for Entrance: Bees that do not belong to the colony try to get into the hive to be accepted by the colony.

Birthing Cell: A cell that the queen lays an egg in.

Bottom Bar: The bottom bar of a frame in a Langstroth beehive.

Bottom Board: Floor of a man-made beehive.

Bottom Insert: Material that is inserted into the hive during the winter months and then removed in the spring, along with the debris collected all winter.

Brace Comb: Comb that is built between the frames of a hive.

Breeding Stock: Larvae and eggs that are picked for particular traits from specific colonies when breeding future queens.

Brood: Young bees in any stage: eggs, larvae, and pupae.

Brood Chamber: The area in the hive where the colony's brood is housed.

Brood Nest: Every comb in the colony that contains brood.

Burr Comb: A comb built in between two parallel combs.

C

Capped Brood: Time between pupa and adult when a cell is capped.

Cappings: The thin beeswax top on cells filled with pure honey.

Capping Scratcher: An uncapping fork; also called a capping scratcher.

Carniolan: Gentle, dark-colored species of bees originating from the Carniolan Alps.

Castes: Name for the different types of bees: queen, worker, drone.

Caucasian: Dark-gray European bees that have excessive use of propolis.

Cell: A hexagonal partition in a honeycomb that bees build to raise brood and to store honey, pollen, and water.

Cellar Detention: This is the act of keeping mating boxes and artificial swarms in a cool room at about 60°F for up to two days to give the bees a chance to get used to the new queen.

Chalk Brood: A fungal disease that affects the larvae of honey bees.

Chilled Brood: A brood killed by cold temperatures.

Cleansing Flight: A short flight for the purpose of voiding waste products. During the winter, the waste stays in the colon, and when spring arrives, the bees take a cleansing flight to void all waste.

Cluster: Bees gathered close together for warmth in temperatures of 55°F or colder.

Colony: Adult bees, brood, and hive all comprise the colony.

- *Development of Colonies*: The phase during which brood are normally raised beginning with the winter rest and coming to a head during the summer solstice.

- *Drone Colony*: A colony with too many drones.

- *Queenless Colony*: A colony without a queen.

- *Queenright Colony*: A colony that has a queen.

- *Uniting Colonies*: The act of taking weak colonies and joining them to make strong colonies.

Comb: Beeswax shaped into six-sided cells that will be filled with honey, pollen, or brood.

Comb Foundation: Man-made sheets of plastic with pre-set cells embedded.

Comb Honey: Honey sold with the comb.

Comb Pliers: Tools to work the hive from the backside.

Comb Settling: On occasion, when moved to a new hive the bees will move out because it does not feel like home. Comb settling occurs when they stay in the new hive and consider it home.

Compound Eyes: Bee's eyes made of small sight organs called ommatidia.

Crawling: Bees will crawl when unable to fly because of acarine disease, varroatosis, or poisoning.

Crimped Wire Foundation: Crimped wire vertically embedded in the foundation of a honeycomb.

Crystallization: The granulation of honey from liquid to solid.

D

Dancing: The communication movements of a bee when relaying information such as food sources and locations of perspective homes.

Dearth: The absence of nectar, pollen, or other food.

Debris: The small bits of wax that have fallen to the hive floor as the bees chew off the comb cappings of brood and honey cells.

Decoy Hive: A hive used to attract swarming bees away from their former hive.

Deep Hive Body: Often called the brood box; specifically used for the queen and brood rearing.

Dividing: Separating a single hive to make two individual colonies.

Division Board Feeder: Feeding apparatus shaped like a frame.

Double Screen: Two layers of wire screen between a wooden frame that is ½- to ¾-inch thick, used to separate two colonies within the same hive, stacked on top of each other with an entrance on the top and the rear of the hive for the upper colony.

Drawn Comb: When bees have used an artificial foundation to create their cells.

Drifting: When hives are close together and bees lose their sense of direction and wander into foreign hives.

Drone: The male honey bee.

Drone Brood: The male honey bee in an immature state.

Drone Comb: A specific area of the comb that is designated for rearing drone brood. The cells in drone comb are convex and larger than worker bee cells.

Drone Congregation Area: Where drones gather to mate with queens.

Drone Killing: When the worker bees force out the drones after the reproductive season is over.

Drone Layer: A phenomenon that occurs when the queen is infertile and lays unfertilized eggs that develop into drones. The queen is then a drone layer.

Dummy Frame: A section of wood cut to resemble a frame in a hive.

E

Early Flow Area: An area where the honey flow comes earlier than in the rest of the country, basically from March through July.

Egg: Stage One of a bee's metamorphoses. The egg is tiny, clear, and shaped like a comma when first laid.

End Bars: Frame pieces that fit between the top and bottom bars.

Entrance: Where the bees go in and out of the hive.

Entrance Reducer: A device used to restrict the size of the entrance to make it easier for the bees to defend against robber bees and other pests.

European Foulbrood: A bacterial disease that a healthy hive might be able to control; also responds to chemical treatment. Not as serious as American foulbrood.

Extractor: A machine that removes honey from combs by spinning the comb. Honey harvested this way is called extracted or liquid honey.

Excluder Grid: A section of material inserted in the hive between the brood box and the honey supers with small spaces just large enough for the worker bees to pass through, but not the queen.

F

Fall Feeding: Feeding the hive in the fall months by artificial means.

Fanning: When the bees ventilate the hive by beating their wings very fast at the entrance and deeper inside the hive to help control temperature and moisture evaporation for curing honey. A separate type of fanning is used for communication when bees release and fan the scent from the Nasonov gland to help foraging bees find their way back home.

Feral Bees: Wild honey bees not kept in a man-made beehive.

Fermentation: What happens when honey has a high moisture content and ferments with yeast.

Fertile Queen: A mated queen that lays fertilized eggs.

Field Bee: A bee that has been given the job of collecting nectar.

Flower Fidelity: The tendency of bees to stay with one particular flower on each foraging trip.

Flying Bees: Bees that have become old enough to fly from the hive and take on foraging tasks; around 3 weeks old.

Foundation: Sheet of beeswax with cell shapes embossed on it to give bees a headstart building their comb.

Frame: A rectangle of wooden pieces that fits in a super and used to hold honeycomb and brood.

Frame Runner: A metal part of the hive body that supports the frames as they hang. The metal is folded and fastened to the upper end, inside of the hive.

Frame Spacer: Pieces of plastic or metal put in the hive to make spaces for supers and frames. They fit over the frame lugs and touch the spacer on the next frame.

Fructose: Also called levulose, it is the principal simple sugar in honey.

G

Glucose: One of two main sugars that make up honey.

Granulation: The natural formation of crystals in honey when dextrose reaches a cool temperature.

Guard Bees: Bees that guard the entrance of the hive to prevent unwanted visitors. These bees give off a pheromone that alerts the other bees.

H

Hefting: Lifting a hive in order to judge the weight.

Hive: A home for bees.

Hive Stand: A stand that the beehive sits on for support and to raise it off the ground.

Hive Tool: A metal tool used by beekeepers for use in hive maintenance.

Hoffman Frame: One of a few different types of self-spacing frames.

Honey: The product of the honey bee that has been processed into a thick, sweet syrup.

Honey Bound: When a queen is unable to lay eggs because all the cells in her hive are filled with honey.

Honeycomb: Comb made by bees that are filled with honey.

Honey Extractor: A machine that removes honey from the frames.

Honey Flow: When a profusion of nectar is available for foraging bees.

Honey House: A beekeeper's workshop where tools are stored; also a place where honey is extracted and stored.

Honey Ripener: A honey holding tank that lets air bubbles rise to the surface before they are expelled.

House Bee: A worker bee that stays in the hive and performs chores such as cleaning, feeding, brood care, and taking care of nectar that foraging bees bring in.

I

Inner Cover: The wooden piece that fits between the outer cover and the hive body in a beehive.

Integrated Pest Management (IPM): Scientific approach used to curb pest infestation.

Invert Sugar Syrup: Sucrose that has been broken down into equal parts of glucose and fructose.

L

Larva: The second stage of a bee's metamorphosis.

Laying Worker: A worker that lays drone eggs when the colony becomes queenless.

Levulous: Also known as fructose, this is one of the two simple sugars that make up honey.

M

Mandible: A bee's mouth part that resembles two arm-like jaws.

Mating Flight: The flight the virgin queen takes to mate with drones while in mid-air.

Mead: An alcoholic drink made from fermented honey and water.

Melomel: Mead made with honey and fruit juice.

Metal Ends: Same as frame spacers. They are added to the hive frames to space them a desired length apart.

Metal Runner: Same as frame runners. They hold the frames in the desired position.

Migratory Beekeeping: Moving a colony from place to place during the honey flow season to take advantage of several different flows.

Miller Feeder: A bee feeder made of wood that is the same size as the hive.

Modified National: The most common beehive used in the United Kingdom.

Mouseguard: A strip of sturdy material, like wood or metal, placed in front of the hive entrance to block mice.

N

Nectar: The sugar-rich product of flowering plants that bees use to make honey.

Nectar Guide: Distinctive marks on plants and flowers that are believed to direct bees to nectar.

Nosema: A mite that usually infects adult bees through their digestive system, causing dysentery and death, if not treated.

Nucleus Hive: A colony so small that it only lives on three to five frames; it is also used to maintain a queen or start a new colony.

Nurse Bee: A bee in charge of feeding and caring for the brood.

O

Orientation Flight: The first flight young bees take before than begin to forage.

Out-apiary: Apiaries that are kept away from the apiarist's home.

Ovary: An egg-producing organ found in the queen and worker bees; highly developed in the queen and under-developed in the workers.

P

Petiole: The area of a bee's body between the abdomen and thorax that serves as its waist.

Pheromone: Considered an external hormone; a scent used in a variety of ways, from attracting to warning.

Pollen: A fine-to-coarse powder that consists of grains that produce the male sperm cell of seed plants.

Pollen Basket: A bag-like appendage on bees' back legs that they fill with pollen and water to bring back to the hive.

Pollen Load: The pollen that is in a bee's pollen basket when it arrives at the hive entrance.

Pollination: The act of transferring pollen from the male to the female parts of the plant.

Porter Bee Escape: A device with two spring valves that allows bees to enter one way and exit the other way. It is used to clear bees out of supers.

Prime Swarm: The first swarm that leaves the hive with the old queen.

Propolis: A substance bees collect from trees and plants that they use in their hives for covering cracks and crevices, or dead bees and other intruders.

Pupa: The third phase of a bee's life. During this time, the organs develop into an adult bee's organs.

Q

Queen: A female bee larger and longer than the other bees; she has highly developed reproductive organs and is the mother of the colony.

Queen Cell: A cell that is larger than others and fit to hold a queen.

Queen excluder: A device that keeps the queen in one part of the hive.

Queen Substance: Pheromones the queen uses to control her colony.

Queenless: When the colony is without a queen.

Queenright: A colony that has a strong, healthy queen who performs all her duties and contributes to the good health of the colony.

R

Robbing: When bees from a foreign colony rob honey that they did not make. Sometimes wasps and other insects will rob from the hive as well.

Royal Jelly: Worker bees secrete royal jelly from glands in their head and use it to feed bees.

S

Sacbrood: A virus that kills larvae in their final stages of maturation.

Scout Bee: A worker bee that goes out to look for food, water, nectar, or a new location for a swarming colony.

Sealed Brood: The time of a bee's development during the pupa stage.

Sections: Bass wood frames with honeycomb already built in, or a plastic form that has honeycomb built in.

Self-Spacing Frame: A beehive frame where the top-most part of the side bar stretches to touch the frame next to it.

Skep: A straw beehive without frames. They are no longer used as hives, but only as a device for collecting swarms.

Small Hive Beetle (SHB): A small beetle that enters the hive to eat honey and pollen. It is black, brown, or dark red with strange fringed antennae.

Smoke: Used in beekeeping as a way to calm and disorient the bees.

Smoker: A device used to burn organic materials such as wood or dry grass. It is also used to calm and disorient the bees.

Spermatheca: One of the queen bee's internal organs that allows her to hold sperm received from drones while on her mating flight.

Spiracles: An opening on the sides of the thorax and abdomen that leads to the bee's breathing tubes.

Stinger: The female bee's defense mechanism. It is a barbed, sharp needle used to distribute a poison into the predator.

Stone Brood: A disease caused by fungi that turns the brood to hard, chalky substances.

Stores: Honey that is stored and used to feed the colony during the winter.

Super: The boxes that make up the beehive; designed to typically hold 10 frames.

Supercedure: Natural replacement of a queen.

Sugar Water: A mixture of water and sugar used to feed bees.

Swarm: A flying collection of bees that leave their hive with their queen en route to a new location.

Swarm Cell: Queen cell found on the bottom of combs, indicating a plan to swarm.

Swarm Prevention: Various methods apiarists use to stop the bees from swarming.

T

Thin Foundation: A foundation sheet that is most often used for production of comb honey.

Thorax: The central part of a bee's body that contains the wings and legs.

Tropilaelaps: Parasitic mites that can affect brood and adult bees; they are similar to the varroa mites. Its usual and most natural host is the Asian honey bee, but it can adapt to other colonies easily.

U

Uncapping Knife: A knife used during honey extraction to scrape off the wax cappings of the honey cells.

Uniting: Forming a larger colony by combining two or more colonies into one. This most often happens when one colony is weak or has lost its queen.

V

Varroa Mites: A serious threat to the health of a colony. Mites are incubated in brood cells and cause deformation and death. They can also be found attached to a healthy adult bee; they eventually cause death.

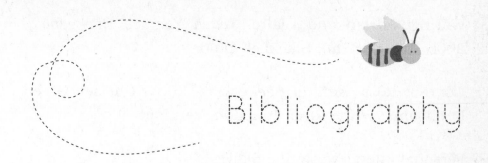

Bibliography

www.honeybeequiet.com/beehive7.html (industry).

www.setiai.com/archives/000067.html (neurons).

Anies Hannawati Purnamadjaja and R. Andrew Russell. "Pheromone communication in a robot swarm: necrophoric bee behavior and its replication," 2005. Robotica, 23, pp. 731-742 doi:10.1017/S0263574704001225.

Blackiston, Howland. *Beekeeping For Dummies,* 2002. Wiley Publishing, Inc.; Hoboken, New Jersey.

Flottum, Kim. *The Backyard Beekeeper,* 2005. Quarry Books; Beverly, Maine.

Melzer, Werner. *Beekeeping: A Complete Owner's Manual,* 1989. Barrons Books; Munich, West Germany.

Cambridge University Press.

Waring, Adrian and Claire. *Teach Yourself Beekeeping*, 2006. McGraw-Hill; Blacklick Ohio.

Conrad, Ross. *Natural Beekeeping*, 2007. Chelsea Green Publishing; White River Junction, Vermont.

Personal interview: Cathie Skove.

Personal interview: Lynda Cook Rizzardi.

Personal interview: Howland Blackiston.

Personal interview: Ilse Ackermann.

Personal interview: Ed Colby.

Personal interview: Charles Parton.

Person interview: Jason Gropple.

Author Biography

Cindy Belknap is a licensed Florida beekeeper and a member of the Alachua County Beekeepers Club and the Florida State Beekeepers Association.

About the association

Established in March 2009, the Alachua County Beekeepers Club is the second largest regional beekeepers group in Florida. The mission of the club is to educate the public of all aspects involving honey bees and other pollinators endangered through chemical use, diseases, parasites, or other problems encountered in a bee's short lifespan. We encourage new beekeepers by assisting them in setup and operation of hives throughout the first year, and to assist all members as needed. We also encourage the youth of the area to become involved in saving our honey bees.

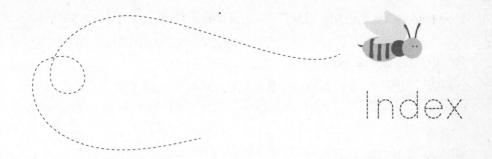

Index

Beeautiful Photos
from Professional Beekeepers

Busy as a bee

Honey bee with varroa mite

Close up view of varroa mite

Honey bee on the comb

Enlarged photo of trachea mites found in the bee trachea

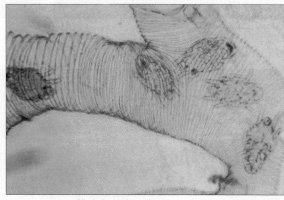

All photographs on this page are provided by the USDA

Beehives and feeders

Lakeside Apiary

Provided by FDACS-DPI (University of Florida)

Inspecting the hive

Provided by Amy Grisak

Beehive placed for pollination

Provided by Amy Grisak

Unprotected winter hives

Provided by Amy Grisak

Depositing a captured swarm in a hive

Backyard hives

Honey bees spilling out of hive

Beehives set up for fruit tree pollination

Beehive with a front feeder

Bees in nucs

All photographs on this page provided by Amy Grisak

Smoking the hive

Provided by Carmen Borthwick

Pollination and flowers

Honey bee on a raspberry blossom

Both photos provided by Amy Grisak

Provided by Carmen Borthwick

Provided by the USDA

Working with bees

Capturing a swarm

A happy beekeeper and her new hives

Provided by Amy Grisak

Provided by Amy Grisak

Requeening a colony

Beekeepers looking for the queen

Inspecting the apiary

All photographs on this page are provided by the USDA

Cemetery hives

Wax moth larvae and dead honey bees

Brood frame

All photographs on this page are provided by FDACS-DPI (University of Florida)

Hive frame loaded with bees

Provided by FDACS-DPI (University of Florida)

Inspector checking the hive with the beekeeper

Provided by USDA

Making honey

Provided by Carmen Borthwick

Provided by Carmen Borthwick

Uncapping the honey cells

Ready for judging

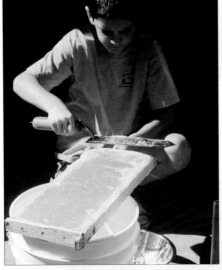

Provided by Amy Grisak

Provided by Amy Grisak

Honey pouring into filter bucket

Frames spinning in extractor

Provided by Amy Grisak

Provided by Amy Grisak

Just bees

Queen bee in a shipping cage

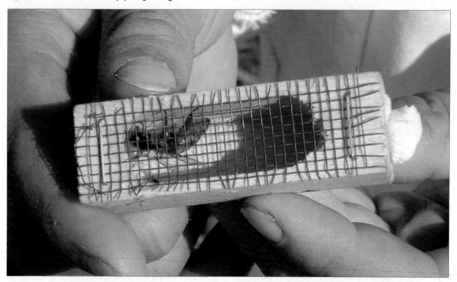

Swarm gathering to move to their new home

All photographs on this page are provided by Amy Grisak

Small swarm on a lilac

Bees inspecting the brood

Bees caring for their brood

All photographs on this page are provided by Carmen Borthwick

Honey bee

Provided by FDACS-DPI (University of Florida)

Frame covered with bees

Provided by Carmen Borthwick

Honey bee coming in for a landing

Provided by FDACS-DPI (University of Florida)

Taking care of the brood

Provided by FDACS-DPI (University of Florida)

Building and equipment

Assembling frames

Provided by Amy Grisak

Old-time smokers

Provided by FDACS-DPI (University of Florida)

Historical

Trucks being loaded with commercial beehives

Packing up for a trip

Inspecting the frame

Certifying Tupelo honey

Burning hives with foulbrood

All historical photographs are provided by FDACS-DPI (University of Florida)